GUERRILLA NETWORKING

A PROVEN BATTLE PLAN TO ATTRACT THE VERY PEOPLE YOU WANT TO MEET

JAY CONRAD LEVINSON

FATHER OF GUERRILLA MARKETING WITH OVER 14 MILLION BOOKS SOLD

AND MONROE MANN

COMBAT VETERAN AND FOUNDER, UNSTOPPABLE ARTISTS, THE
JUGGERNAUT CLUB, AND AMERICAN BREAK DIVING ASSOCIATION

NEW YORK

GUERRILLA NETWORKING

By Jay Conrad Levinson & Monroe Mann
© 2008 Jay Conrad Levinson, Guerrilla Marketing
International & Monroe Mann. All rights reserved.

ISBN: 978-1-60037-016-8   Paperback

ISBN: 978-1-60037-019-9   eBook

Published by:

MORGAN · JAMES
THE ENTREPRENEURIAL PUBLISHER™

Morgan James Publishing, LLC
1225 Franklin Ave Ste 325
Garden City, NY 11530-1693
Toll Free 800-485-4943
www.MorganJamesPublishing.com

Cover and Inside Design by:
Heather Kirk
www.GraphicsByHeather.com
Heather@GraphicsByHeather.com

Habitat
for Humanity®
Peninsula
Building Partner

TRADITIONAL NETWORKING:

"Meeting People"

GUERRILLA NETWORKING:

"Becoming the type of person OTHER people want to meet"

THE BOTTOM LINE:

Guerrilla networking does NOT mean meeting people.
It means becoming the type of person other people want to meet.

Guerrilla networking does NOT mean who you know or who knows you.
It means who thinks highly enough of you to take your phone calls.

Guerrilla networking does NOT mean schmoozing.
It means becoming the type of person other people want to schmooze with.

Guerrilla networking does NOT mean a huge rolodex.
It means becoming the type of person other people add to their rolodex.

Guerrilla networking does NOT mean 'getting out there.'
It means becoming the type of person other people invite out.

Guerrilla networking does NOT mean handing out business cards.
It means being so famous and successful that you don't need a business card.

Guerrilla networking does NOT mean crashing parties.
It means being the host of parties that other people want to crash.

Guerrilla networking does NOT mean finding investors.
It means developing projects that everyone else wants to invest in.

Guerrilla networking does NOT mean dating.
It means becoming the type of person that everyone else wants to date.

Guerrilla networking does NOT mean becoming involved in others projects.
It means starting projects that everyone else wants to be involved with.

Guerrilla networking does NOT mean meeting people.
It means becoming the type of person that other people want to meet.

www.StopMeetingPeople.com

ABOUT THE AUTHORS

Jay Conrad Levinson is the author of the best-selling marketing series in history, *"Guerrilla Marketing,"* plus 44 other business books. His books have sold 15 million copies worldwide. And his guerrilla concepts have influenced marketing so much that his books appear in 43 languages and are required reading in MBA programs worldwide.

Jay taught guerrilla marketing for 10 years at the extension division of the University of California in Berkeley. He was a practitioner of it in the United States — as Senior VP at J. Walter Thompson, and in Europe, as Creative Director of Leo Burnett Advertising. A winner of first prizes in all the media, he has been part of the creative teams that made household names of many of the most famous brands in history: The Marlboro Man, The Pillsbury Doughboy, Allstate's good hands, United's friendly skies, and the Sears Diehard battery.

Jay has written for *Entrepreneur Magazine, Inc. Magazine*, and the Microsoft Website. He is the Chairman of Guerrilla Marketing International. His Guerrilla Marketing empire includes a series of books, workshops, CDs, videos, a CD-ROM, a radio show, a series of podcasts, an Internet larkmark, and The Guerrilla Marketing Association — a support system for small business. Guerrilla Marketing is a way for business owners to spend less, get more, and achieve substantial profits. To transform you into a marketing guerrilla, there is no better person than "The Father of Guerrilla Marketing" — Jay Conrad Levinson. More info:

www.GMarketing.com

www.GuerrillaMarketingAssociation.com

JayView@aol.com

Phone: 415-453-2162

Monroe Mann is the founder of Unstoppable Artists, LLC, the world's only business, marketing, and financial strategic firm for actors, directors, authors, and artists. He has helped his clients sign to major agencies, publish books, star in their own films and plays, play in their own bands, raise funds, buy homes, invest their money, and in general, just become really successful. Students/clients have appeared in/on *People Magazine, Inside Edition, Entrepreneur, Entertainment Tonight, CNN, ABC News, Variety, Hollywood Reporter, Backstage, Boston Globe, Glamour, Keith Ablow, NY Times*, and the list goes on.

Monroe is also the CEO of Loco Dawn Films, LLC; a graduate of Hollywood Film Institute and Digital Film Academy; a SAG, AFTRA, EQUITY actor listed on IMDb; the lead singer of the seven-piece ROMP band, Running for Famous; and the screenwriter, executive producer, and co-star of a number of films, including the upcoming wakeboarding feature, *In the Wake*, with music by

Avril Lavigne and Sum41. Monroe is proud to be a certified Guerrilla Marketing coach; the recipient of a business degree from Franklin College in Switzerland; a graduate student at Lubin School of Business, Pace Law School, and Western Carolina University's Master of Entrepreneurship program; and a combat veteran of Operation Iraqi Freedom. He is also the author of a number of critically acclaimed books, including *The Theatrical Juggernaut – The Psyche of the Star*; *Battle Cries for the Underdog*; *To Benning & Back*; and the upcoming *The Artist's MBA*. Finally, he is the founder of the international networking action group called, "The Juggernaut Club" (send him an email about it), and the founder of the American Break Diving Association.

For those who are completely obsessed with success and are ready to take control of their circumstances once and for all, he is available for private business coaching (face-to-face in Manhattan; by phone internationally) and encourages you to contact him to set up a **FREE** 20-minute career consultation by phone. He is also available to speak at your organization. More info:

www.UnstoppableArtists.com, www.LocoDawn.com, www.TheJClub.net, www.BreakDiving.com, www.FutureOscarWinner.com, www.IMDb.com

MonroeMann@AOL.com or Roe@UnstoppableArtists.com

Phone: 646-764-1764

ACKNOWLEDGEMENTS

FROM MONROE MANN

Thank you to Jay Levinson for making this possible. You are one of my heroes and to think that you agreed to co-write this book with me: I am still trying to catch my breath from the honor and privilege! There have been so many people who have doubted me, ridiculed me, and told me I was going to fail in my 29 ripe years; in a sea of such negativity, you were, and continue to be, the sweetest breath of fresh air I have yet to encounter, and one of my greatest supporters. Thank you for your faith and steadfast optimism, and for your unyielding support of my dreams.

Thank you to the US Army and Uncle Sam for deploying me to Iraq. Had you not done so, I never would have been inspired to get in touch with Jay in the first place. You are responsible for this book coming to be.

Thank you to every soldier, sailor, marine, airman, and coastie who served 'by my side' in Iraq and Afghanistan.

To those who never made it home, I shed a tear every day in humble gratitude for your sacrifice for my freedom. I love you, will never forget you, and dedicate every one of my successes to you — to you who have given your life in order to make mine possible.

Thanks to Hilary Duff, Avril Lavigne, and Rachel Bilson for helping me survive the war — I look forward to finally thanking you in person.

Thank you to Mitch Meyerson, Al Lautenslager, Jeannie Levinson, Amy Levinson, Daniel Huffman, and the rest of the team at Guerrilla Marketing International.

Thank you to my brilliant friends and business associates — Ned Vizzini, Andrew Young, Carol Blaha, Arthur Brown, James Dillehay, Barry Morgenstein, Kathy Hagenbuch, Debbie Bordelon, Graham Guerra, Ashley Ann Serafin, Knox Vanderpool, Paul Rieckhoff, Bones Rodriguez, Dennis Hurley, Phil Malandrino, Douglas C. Williams, Roberta Muse, Kip Gienau, Marcia Harp, Scott duPont, Kolie Crutcher, Ed Smith, Scott Norman, and Peter Bielagus — for your generous contributions to this book: your guerrilla networking stories have added so much to the project, and I thank you for your assistance. To the top!

And leaving the best for last, thank you to God, Jesus, Carolyn, Monroe Sr., Emily, Hilary, and all others who have supported me on my journey. Jesus especially: he's a real cool cat, and someone I definitely look forward to meeting!

FROM JAY CONRAD LEVINSON

Because Monroe did the tough parts of creating this book, I can understand why his acknowledgements were overflowing with gratitude to a host of people. Thank you, Monroe, for making me one of them.

My only acknowledgements for the book readers hold in their hands go to three people:

David Hancock, the perfect publisher for an entrepreneurial work of this quality and depth; Monroe Mann, who had the vision and then was able to write a delightfully readable book that conveys that vision clearly and passionately; and my wife, Jeannie, the best possible result of guerrilla networking.

TABLE OF CONTENTS

PREFACE

Networking does NOT mean meeting people. That definition is just plain wrong, and it's no wonder why so many entrepreneurs feel lost when it comes to networking—which should actually be very easy. You see, networking should be easy, and *is* easy. The key to your success simply lies in which definition of networking your subscribe to.

Networking does not mean 'meeting people.' Actually, it means, 'becoming the type of person that *other* people want to meet.'

For example, take some of the big movers and shakers in business, such as Bill Gates, Tony Hawk, and Avril Lavigne. They have taken the power of networking to its highest level: people want to meet *them*.

Ask yourself this question: would people stand in line for hours to meet with either of these three entrepreneurs? Yes! Why? The answer is simple. They know how to network, for they became the type of person that *other* people want to meet.

This same networking principle applies to dating, friendship, and yes, small business. Why work your butt off to meet people when you can put that same energy into becoming an interesting person within your field, and then, benefit again by having the same people you want to meet... *come up to you?*

Herein lies the power of this principle: you kill two birds with one stone. While your boring competition — who no one wants to meet — is out there desperately trying to meet people day after day, you, on the other hand, are actively putting your efforts into becoming as cool as humanly possible.

By diversifying your offerings, be becoming a leader in your field, and by putting together a knock out marketing angle, you'll end up taking your industry by storm.

The result: your competition, the press, and customers alike end up at your doorstep, trying to meet *you*.

To the uninformed, this public interest might appear to be a lucky fluke. You, however, would know that it was actually the result of your persistent hard work, and the fruit of your foolproof guerrilla networking plan finally reaping its reward: you became the type of person/business that *other* people wanted to meet and work with.

If you continually try to 'meet people,' especially without changing and improving your marketing angle along the way, you're wasting time. Meeting people can do nothing for you if you yourself have nothing interesting to offer.

Taken further, you might have noticed that no one wants you to tell them how wonderful you are; people want to discover and find that out for themselves. And therein lies another key to guerrilla networking: your accomplishments are not as impressive if you have to tell people about them yourself.

Bottom line: if you're playing your networking cards right, and are out there *doing interesting things* in the public eye, people should be flocking to meet you. You should be receiving emails, phone calls, and letters from those who think you (and your company) are so cool, that they want to do business with you. If not, it's because you're not memorable enough to warrant such action, in which case, you better re-evaluate your guerrilla networking strategy immediately!

So remember: networking does not mean meeting people; it means becoming the type of person other people want to meet. Become as cool as possible, get your brand out there as much as possible, and let us find out for ourselves how cool you are.

In other words, don't necessarily try to meet us; the idea is to make us want to meet you. And if you're reading this book, yes, you're probably someone who we want to meet.

~*Monroe & Jay*

FOREWORD

GUERRILLA NETWORKING IN ACTION BY A TRUE GUERRILLA
BY JAY CONRAD LEVINSON

I'm the kind of guy who answers almost all email so when I got one from someone named Monroe Mann who was heading to Iraq, I was fascinated.

Monroe had also sent me a book he had written called *The Theatrical Juggernaut – The Psyche of the Star*. I was double fascinated. Of the more than 300 business books in this house, only two are kept by my word processor... and one is Monroe's.

We began a correspondence and the fertility of his mind blew mine away. This young man had a lot of plans and was able to breathe life into all of them even in the face of adversity and long odds... most notably no connections in publishing, show business, and then a deployment to Iraq.

I was impressed. I invited Monroe to be a guest on a weekly tele-call that is held for guerrilla marketers. Monroe's personality, content, earnestness and sense of humor made him the best-liked speaker of the year — and he wasn't even prepared to speak.

In that hour, and then further over the course of a bunch of emails that he sent from Iraq, he managed to prove to me his powers of communication. Therefore, when he asked if we might do a book together, it was a cinch to say yes.

Monroe is a living atom of networking, and this book that he has created will give you more than an atom-sized perspective on the subject — truly from the inside out.

I started out as his teacher and have ended up as Monroe's student.

INTRODUCTION

BY MONROE MANN

Perhaps you are wondering how I — 20-something Monroe Mann — connected, hooked up, and become friends with Jay Conrad Levinson? Now *that* is an interesting question, and it truly shows the power of guerrilla networking — a networking philosophy born in my classroom and guerrilla-fied by the magnificent Jay Levinson.

On May 23rd, 2004, I had an office in Union Square, my own business, an up-and coming band, and a feature film in development. I was living out my dreams in full color.

On May 24th, Uncle Sam changed all that with a simple phone call: "Lieutenant Mann, your National Guard unit has been mobilized. You're going to Iraq."

Literally overnight, my perspective on life was changed forever. Oh my God! I'm going to war! Oh my God, I'm leaving everything I've ever known behind! Oh my God, I might very well die over there!

That last part really got to me: I might never come home! What an odd feeling to have, to say the least. The thought that I might never see my family or my friends again was horrible. Then I began thinking about all the things I wish I had done, but never got around to doing. So, now on top of being depressed, I was feeling guilty too!

One of those 'things' that I wished I had done was to thank my hero and mentor, Jay Conrad Levinson, author of the famous *Guerrilla Marketing* series of books (with over 15 million copies sold in over 43 languages!) It began to occur to me that not only could I die in Iraq (bad enough), but that I might end up dying without ever speaking to, thanking, or getting to know Jay Conrad Levinson — the man who helped me realize that I was an entrepreneur in the first place (even worse)!

So I made a decision: *now* was time to thank him. And in order to do that, I needed to get in touch with him. But how?

I went to his website at <u>www.GMarketing.com</u> and scoured for a personal phone number. A mailing address. His personal email address. Nothing! All I could find was an email address for his webmaster! Arghh! I was so frustrated. Darn these celebrities!

But I was on a mission. And I had nothing to lose. And this webmaster's email address was all I had to go on. I had to make an effort. Even if he didn't read what I sent, and even if he didn't respond, I had to at least *try* to relate my gratitude to this angel of a man.

So, I took 10 minutes and drafted an email. I told Jay what an influence he had been, that I was being sent to Iraq, and that I wanted to thank him now — in case I never returned from the war — and reminded him that I included him in the acknowledgements of the first book I had published called, *The Theatrical Juggernaut – The Psyche of the Star.* Years earlier, I had sent a complimentary copy of that book to him, but I was sure he had never read it. Heck, I wasn't even sure if he had ever even received it.

I thought to myself: What am I doing, trying to send an email to the *father* of Guerrilla Marketing, through his webmaster no less, and expecting him to actually read the email, let alone respond. Ha! What a joke. How deluded can I get? Who the heck am I to think Jay would respond to me?

A moment later, I pressed 'Send.' Heck, ya never know, right? And that was pretty much the last 'communication' with Jay Conrad Levinson that I thought I would ever have.

Well… the next day, I checked my email. And I had perhaps the biggest double-take of my life. Is this a joke? This can't be! Is this for real? IS THIS FOR REAL?!

I was looking in disbelief at an email from none other than the man himself: Jay Conrad Levinson. AN EMAIL FROM JAY CONRAD LEVINSON! Oh my God! I'll be honest—I screamed. I was jumping up and down. Sitting in my inbox, quietly staring out at me, was a name that just took my breath away. It remains to this day one of the highlights of my life: my hero just wrote me an email! *Never know* indeed!

But the words inside that email were what really made an impression: "Monroe. There are 31 books on my computer desk bookshelf. 30 are those I have written. And the other? *The Theatrical Juggernaut* by Monroe Mann. You're a heckuva talented writer, Monroe. – Jay"

Wow! This was unbelievable! What is going on?!

A week later, I was being interviewed live on his Guerrilla Marketing teleclass. Soon thereafter, I became his e-pal. And thus began an email friendship that grew stronger and stronger during my 18-months of active duty (to include the final 11 in Iraq.) I even discovered that Mr. Levinson himself — like me — was at one point an intelligence officer in the United States Army. I was floored. Hooah, Jay!

So, we kept in contact with each other throughout the next 18 months, and towards the end of my tour — heck, I had just about survived through an entire war — I decided to go for broke. My new mission: get Jay to write a book with me before I return to the United States.

Sure, he had been helping me greatly with my marketing through-out my time in Iraq as I prepared for my return back to the States, and giving me hints and tips from a business plan standpoint, but what I always dreamed about was co-authoring a book with the great father of Guerrilla Marketing himself; with the gentleman responsible for creating my own obsession for marketing.

Well, as I learned from his response to my initial email... *ya never know!* SO TRY. And I did.

Truthfully, the fear of what he might say in response to my question seemed worse than the enemy fire in Iraq. But I stayed strong; stayed focused on the mission at hand; and after writing up a concise pitch proposing five different books, my trigger finger made the gutsiest move of my combat deployment: it clicked my request into the annals of history.

Low and behold (I'm still in shock), one of my ideas piqued his interest. His response? 'Guerrilla Networking. Let's do that one.' That was it. Short, sweet, to the point, and well, that's all I needed to hear.

One of my lifelong dreams had just become a reality.

I had managed to propel my entire career forward *from a combat zone*.

And all of a sudden, living in a cloth tent in the brutally hot deserts of Iraq with mortars and rockets raining down on top of me — well, somehow, it just didn't seem so bad anymore.

Thanks again Jay.

****

The point of us telling you these stories (of how we connected) is that they illustrate how the two of us both have utilized the principles of guerrilla networking in our own lives and careers. Jay became the type of person I wanted to meet and work with. I became the type of person that Jay wanted to meet and work with.

Our 'connection' had little to do with the fact that one wanted to meet the other; the power lied in the fact that each of us had become the person the *other* wanted to meet.

Our ultimate mission was not to meet people, but rather, to become the type of person others wanted to meet.

It is precisely because of that philosophy in action — because of guerrilla networking — that you are reading this book today. The philosophy works.

We hope you benefit from it as much as we have. Enjoy!

WHAT IS THIS BOOK?

BY MONROE MANN

This book is SIMPLE. A simple concept and a simple premise. This is a book of ideas, based on one unifying concept that we are going to be repeating over and over again ad nauseam in this book: networking is becoming the type of person that *other* people want to meet.

Go back and read that last sentence. *That* is what this book is about, and that is the entire focus of every page that follows. This entire book's purpose is to help you simply understand the profound truth of that statement: that you will meet more influential people if you spend more time focusing on *becoming* an influential person to begin with.

If you look around you, most of the people you see on a daily basis are not really remarkable in any standout way, or they certainly aren't telling you otherwise.

Well, that's the key. Most people are *not* curiously attractive. Most people, businesses, and marketing efforts are so boring, blasé, hackneyed, trite, and unremarkable that they don't succeed, or at the very most, just drag along.

The ideas espoused in this book are designed to help you avoid such a description of your life and/or business.

The mission of this book is to help you become a guerrilla networker; to help you become the very person who other people desperately want to meet.

Years ago, I was an actor in the movie *Swimfan*. I played the role of Jake Donnelly, the comatose ex-boyfriend who 'comes to life' at the end — a small but critical role that earned me my first official credit in a major Hollywood film. But that's all it got me.

You see, I spent my three weeks on set kowtowing to everyone, and desperately trying to schmooze my way into the hearts and minds of the director, producers, and stars, in the erroneous belief that this was my big break and that I had to 'meet' these people if it was the last thing I did.

To an extent, I succeeded. I was invited to barbecues at the producers' homes; I played cards with Jason Ritter, Shiri Appleby, Jesse Bradford, and Erika Christensen; and I even got to the point where I was on a first name basis with director John Polson. But at the end of the shoot, the one line that was being considered for me... was never given to me. And no one from the film became my friend, despite my best efforts. And I realized that I had debased myself, prostituted myself, and wasted three weeks of my life trying to convince people of something that I already knew to be true: I am a great actor, and I am a great guy. Why was I trying so hard to convince them of this?

It was at that moment that I realized my strategy was all wrong. It was also the moment when I realized that perhaps those three weeks on set weren't such a waste after all. You see, I did end up getting my first big credit in a film. More importantly, it was here where the very first seeds of Guerrilla Networking were planted.

Immediately after *Swimfan*, I made a decision: *never again would I spend the majority of my valuable time trying to get cast in films*; from that point forward, I was going to make my OWN breaks. I was going to write my *own* scripts, and produce my *own* movies. The idea? I would just cast *myself* in leading roles! Wait for someone to 'discover' me? Ha! I was going to discover myself.

And what a concept. If I just took all the effort I was using to schmooze my way into other people's projects, and transferred that energy into making my own projects, I would probably see success a lot more quickly. And that's exactly what happened.

From that point on, I was no longer Monroe Mann, mere actor. Now, I had become Monroe Mann, creative and intelligent producer and screenwriter (who also just happened to be an actor). And *that* has made all the difference in the world. I was now a producer. I was suddenly someone that everyone else wanted to meet. And wow of wows, now people wanted me to act in their films as well. Go figure.

Today, I am the executive producer, co-screenwriter, and co-star of the world's first wakeboarding feature film ever, entitled *In the Wake*. Do lots more people want to meet me now because of that? Yes, they do!

Folks — that is what this book is all about: helping **you** to become the type of person other people want to meet. If you embrace what Jay & I share with you here, there's only one way to go, and that's UP!

On that note, I look forward to meeting you... at the top!

NOTE: *Any mention of the word, "I" in the text refers to Monroe Mann. Any reference to, "We" refers to Jay Conrad Levinson & Monroe Mann.*

PART 1

Guerrilla Networking

18

CHAPTER 1:
Networking

Networking according to Merriam Webster's Collegiate Dictionary is defined as, "the exchange of information or services among individuals, groups, or institutions."

That is the problem with most 'networking' strategies. They are based upon a definition that is far too vague, broad, and unspecific to use in daily life and business.

If you search Google for the word 'networking' (as of this date), over 400 million search results come up. Regrettably, almost all of them refer to computer networking, and none to professional networking. When we searched for 'professional networking" (as of this day), 75 million search results came up. Of those on the first results page, all of them refer to and subscribe to a definition of networking that is as equally unclear and unfocused as the definition we find in most dictionaries.

Ask most people the question, "What is networking" and you'll get a variety of answers ranging from 'meeting people' to 'getting your name out there'. Rarely do you receive an answer that actually defines a clear and focused strategy.

The sad truth is that most people give us such vague and cloudy answers because most people truly do not know what networking really means. Even some of the most successful 'networkers' in business can't explain their magical ability of making useful connections because in many cases, even they do not know exactly what it is that they are doing. *(Hint: they are guerrilla networking.)*

Strangely — and this leads us in the direction this book is going — most traditional definitions of networking seem to imply that everyone is already chomping at the bit in anticipation of the day they get the opportunity to meet you — that the hard part is already done — that you are *already* someone who people want to meet.

Regretfully, the reality is anything but. No one cares about you. No one wants to buy from you. No one wants to hang out with you. No one wants to date you. No one wants to be your friend. In fact, no one wants anything to do with you... unless they have already determined for themselves that you are someone that they want to meet. Starting to make sense?

You see, meeting people really just isn't going to do much for you. Meeting people in and of itself is useless. What good is a filled rolodex if those people really don't care about you? The question to ask yourself in such a situation is 'how truly valuable are these contacts?'

Do any of these hundreds of people know who you are? If you called them up on the phone, would they take your call? Would they recognize your name? More importantly, would they drop what they're doing to help you?

Many networking books rattle off suggestions of increasing the number of contacts in your rolodex. We disagree. The quantity of people in your rolodex is second to the quality. It's better to have 11 contacts of quality rather than 10 million in quantity. I would rather have Bill Gates, Steven Spielberg, Jeff Bezos, Hilary Duff, Rudy Giuliani, Gwen Stefani, Conan O'Brian, Billy Joe Armstrong, Jessica Biel, Jessica Alba, and Avril Lavigne as my 10 sole close and personal contacts than have generic and broad connections with all of Hollywood, Washington, and Wall Street. I would rather a small group of people who know me and respect me greatly than a large group of people who really don't know who I am.

And why? Because those 11 people listed above could probably introduce me to anyone else I may want to meet. Quality over quantity is the name of the game. Think about it: if I have the personal cell phone numbers for all those above 11 people in my rolodex — and they in fact knew who I am, respected me, and would always take my calls — then frankly, I could probably get anything done that I dreamed of. Quality over quantity.

So, what defines quality then? A-ha. Therein lies the rub! In our opinion, quality is determined based on one simple thing: their desire to meet you. Does this person truly madly deeply want to meet you? Does this person truly madly deeply want to hear from you? Does this person truly madly deeply believe that he can benefit immeasurably by talking with you? Does this person truly madly deeply believe that time spent with you will be time well spent? Does this person truly madly deeply want to hear your opinion, listen to what you have to say, and ponder what you may have to offer? If the answer to these questions is YES, then that's truly a contact. If the answer to any of these questions is NO, then guess what: this person is not truly a contact. This person is just a name and a phone number on a piece of paper.

Think about this: if your mission is to simply meet people, then just stand outside on the sidewalk in Times Square in New York City and extend your hand to everyone you meet that passes by. One out of three will probably shake your hand, and heck, we'd venture to guess that another one out of nine might actually stop to talk to you.

Mission accomplished, right? Yep! You met people. All day. Congratulations!

You shook their hands. Looked into their eyes. Told them how pleased you were to meet them. And meet them you did. But you really have no idea who they are. And they probably have no idea who you are. And at the end of the day, you are really no better off than when you started. But 'get out there' you did, and boy oh boy did you 'meet people.' You networked, baby! But you didn't sell one more product, one more service, or even entice one of them to want to come back and speak with you again.

This preceding story seems so fanciful and silly and we are sure you are shaking your head, thinking, "Well, of course! But no one would ever do that." And you'd be mistaken! Because that is what 99.9% of the people in this world do when they go to parties. When they go to seminars. When they go on job interviews. When they go out into this brave new world and start 'networking.'

Most people go to parties and hand out business cards. Most people go to seminars and hand out their flyers. Most people go on job interviews and hand out their resumes. Most people go out... and desperately and sickeningly try to *meet people*.

Does no one realize that these marketing tools are simply REMINDER advertising? That these things should not be used as introductions? That these things should be simply used to back up your preceding reputation?

"But I didn't have a preceding reputation," you balk! "No one knew me at that party. And no one knew me at that seminar. And none of these job interviewers knew my name!"

Well, folks, that's precisely the problem. Fortunately, though, that is also exactly the problem that we are going to be helping to solve with you in this book. We are going to help you create that preceding reputation. We are going to help make you so desired that you don't even need to use a business card. So desired that flyers are simply unnecessary. So damn cool that you don't even have to use a resume. That the phone becomes but a simple tool you use only to put to your ear, but never to dial. Sure, you'll still use these traditional tools, *but not as your first line of attack*. Rather, you will use them simply as *reinforcement*.

Which brings us back to the definition of guerrilla networking: becoming the type of person other people want to meet. It is truly a sad state of affairs that even in this day of high technology and the internet, so many people still subscribe to the WRONG and OUTDATED definition of networking; to this idea of 'meeting people.' It is time to change your paradigm and use a new model of networking.

Once and for all, we — the authors of this book — are going to debunk and dethrone this horribly outdated and completely ineffective traditional definition of networking that has kept millions of people from reaching their true potential. Networking does not mean meeting people. We'll say it again: Networking does *not* mean meeting people. One more time, loudly: NETWORKING DOES NOT MEAN MEETING PEOPLE!

No, ladies and gentlemen, networking means becoming the type of person *other* people want to meet. And that's exactly who you are soon going to become.

CHAPTER 2:
Traditional Networking

Before we can better understand what guerrilla networking is all about, our first task is to analyze, dissect, and evaluate 'traditional networking'. This is probably most easily done through the use of an example:

a) We are at a cocktail party.

b) Our subject's name is Francesca.

c) Francesca has one week before the night of the party.

d) No one knows that Francesca is coming to the party, and at this point, no one cares.

If Francesca is a traditional networker, one week prior to the party, this would be her plan. She would:

- Bring lots of business cards that say nothing about what she really does;

- Try to find out who is at the party so she can approach them and hand out her business cards that say nothing about what she really does;

- Tell her friends that she's going to this big party 'to meet people';

- Delude herself into thinking she has a plan, when in fact she really does not;

- And that's basically it.

At the party, she would:

- Come in, and begin the search for the people 'she wants to meet';

- Go on the prowl, moving from one uninterested prospect to another;

- Deposit her business card (that says nothing about what she really does) into each prospect's uninterested hand;

- Bore each prospect so each comes up with some excuse for having to move away;

- Target another prospect, lock in, approach, with business card extended in hand;

- And so it goes for the night.

At the end, Francesca is exhausted. She is smiling because she is certain that at least 45 more people have her business card in hand. She feels accomplished. She feels like she actually should be proud of herself. She thinks she 'made connections' and 'networked like a pro'.

What she doesn't know, though, is what hurts her. If she actually sat down and thought about it, it might occur to her that she really doesn't know much about the people she was speaking with beyond what the general public may know. It might occur to her that most of these people have probably already thrown her business card in the trash because they didn't care about her, or more precisely, because she didn't give them a reason to care. If on the off chance her 'prospects' did keep her card, they probably won't remember her name or face the next day — even if her photo was on her business card. Overall, the night was wasted, and was certainly not as productive as it could have been.

Bottom line, traditional networking is resource heavy, a waste of time, stunts your expansion and development, and more often than not... just does not work. *The problem with traditional networking (among other things) is that you — as the networker — are not developing yourself.* You are simply prancing around trying to get people to want to meet you when instead you should be becoming the type of person people want to meet. Do you note the difference? Telling people that they should want to meet you and get to know just doesn't work. People need to come to this conclusion on their own.

Have you ever approached someone (or seen someone else approach someone) and without really explaining why, just said, "We should hang out." Or what about, "We should do business together." Those phrases are coming from the mouth of a traditional networker. From someone who is assuming that the other person already wants to meet you. Isn't it more powerful if you subtly (or blatantly) give hints and tips that would lead that person you are speaking with to come to that conclusion himself? Isn't that infinitely more powerful?

Truly, think about it. Can you imagine how much more powerful you'd be if those same people came up to you and said those very same things? If those very same people said to you, "Let's go to the movies together." Or, "I have a business proposition for you." You turned the tables and became the type of person they wanted to meet! But alas, we are getting ahead of ourselves. We'll talk more about this later. First, let's return to our discussion of traditional networking: meeting people.

Most people subscribe to this 'old' (and ineffective) definition of networking simply because they do not know of any alternatives. They subscribe to this definition because most of the people they hang out with... KNOW NOTHING OF NETWORKING! If they did, they would stop telling you that networking means, "Meeting people." It most certainly does not, and that is a huge insult to the guerrilla networkers of the world.

Networking does not mean meeting people! Are you starting to get this? Networking does not mean meeting people! Networking does not mean meeting people!

We urge you to reconsider the networking definitions that you yourself have been using. Have you ever really sat down and thought about it? If you did, you might come to the realization that your networking definition is anything but clear, crisp, and defined.

Sure, networking must — of course — help you meet the right people, but far more importantly, in our minds, it must also encourage them to want to meet you **AND** help develop you into a more interesting person as a result. And that is the essence of guerrilla networking: enticing the very people you want to meet into desperately wanting to meet you (by continually becoming a more and more interesting/influential person on a daily basis.)

CHAPTER 3:
Guerrilla Networking

We hope that the previous chapter — chapter two — shook up and debunked the idea of traditional networking enough to encourage you to consider the theory that we are advancing — the theory of guerrilla networking. It is our belief that guerrilla networking (becoming the type of person other people want to meet) is far more effective — and in many ways, easier to implement and reap reward from than traditional networking.

If we want to become successful, the traditional definition of networking just doesn't accomplish what is needed in this competitive world we live in. It's now time to discuss the idea of guerrilla networking in far more detail. And it all begins with the fact that *no one cares who you are.*

In fact, for better or for worse, in this internet driven world we live in these days, no one cares *even more.* Because of the advertising messages we all receive in any given day, we have become an oversaturated society and marketplace. You just *can't* 'meet people' anymore. It just doesn't work! Getting the proverbial 'foot in the door' just doesn't mean anything anymore because the internet has allowed EVERYONE to get their 'foot in the door'. As a result, actually getting your foot in the door today in a meaningful way means doing a lot more than you may have had to do 10 years ago. It's even more difficult to accomplish.

Sure, 10 years ago, maybe 'meeting people' was a viable strategy, but no longer! Things have changed, and it's now a two-step process. Today, you need to not only *get* in that door, but now you need to learn how to *stay* there — because job security is a term that doesn't apply anymore in the brave new world we're living in. That is why guerrilla networking is so important: it helps you stay in the door once you figure out how to get in. More importantly, guerrilla networking is the very tool you need these days just to get invited in the door in the first place!

That being said, you'd be wise to just STOP trying to meet people. Right this very moment. You are wasting your precious time, energy, and resources doing so. Traditional networking just doesn't work anymore (if it even worked to begin with). Just stop dead in your tracks. You need a new strategy.

Good news: the book you are reading is that new strategy. It's called guerrilla networking, and it merely requires a simple (though profound) change in your thinking: becoming the type of person that other people want to meet.

Once this change takes hold of you, your entire way of looking at your career, your business, and your life will change. And once you completely understand it, watch out! Do not underestimate its power. Do not underestimate the power of this one single and solitary principle that we are sharing with you in this book. Those individuals and companies that embrace it are going to become — and stay — very *very* successful. Those who ignore it are going to be bitterly scratching their heads in frustration 10 years from now, wondering why all of the competition (and their very lives) have passed them by.

So, how then does guerrilla networking work in the real world? In order to best illustrate what we mean by guerrilla networking, let's bring back our party crasher Francesca. In the last chapter, she was a traditional networker. In this chapter, she is going to be a guerrilla networker. As such, her entire approach is going to be very very different.

Again, let's assume she has one week prior to the night of the party. Unlike a traditional networker, she would:

- Figure out the type of party this is, and see how she best fits into the needs of this type of party;

- Find out who was going to be at this party, and do everything in her power to 'prepare' them for her arrival by subtly (or blatantly) planting seeds that will sprout on the night of;

- Think of every possible reason why people at this party would, should, or could come up to her, and then plan her strategy accordingly, whether its how she dresses, what she says, who she is with, what she brings with her, etcetera;

- Try to come up with something that could be given to each guest upon their arrival at the party, or upon her arrival — something that would get everyone talking about her (and beyond just a boring business card);

- And this list goes on. Note that this is just her preparation before the party.

On the night of the party, she would:

- Already be expected by most of the guests;

- Have a reputation that precedes her;

- Not be walking around frantically meeting people, but instead, be smiling proudly as everyone at the party walks up to her in order to meet her;

- Give out her business cards after the card is requested, instead of having to shove it down into someone's pocket;

- Be asked to repeat her name, because people want to remember it;

- Be given business cards from everyone at the party, voluntarily, without ever having to ask.

And such is the charmed life of the guerrilla networker.

Is it hard work. You bet! It is incredibly hard work.

Does it involve more preparation and more blood, sweat, and tears in order to get there? You bet it does!

But is it infinitely more effective and rewarding in the long term than 'meeting people'? Absolutely. And therein lies the rub.

You'll note, perhaps, how the tables have in fact turned. When you became a guerrilla networker, the people who wanted to then meet you became... traditional networkers.

You see, traditional networking is not necessarily bad, and in fact, the idea of the 'traditional networker' is never going to completely die. They are simply two sides of the same networking coin. For without traditional networkers, there can be no guerrilla networkers. Does this make sense? The people who want to meet you are the traditional networkers! Yes, when you become a guerrilla networker, and are successful at it, that's what everyone who approaches you inadvertently becomes: a traditional networker! Because they are then trying... to meet you! That is, until they say or do something that makes you want to meet them (in which case now you are the traditional networker.) And so the coin is constantly flipped, one side to the other.

Again we reiterate that traditional networking is *not* always bad. As we just explained, in many cases, you yourself will — and must be — that traditional networker. And in all honesty, in many cases, you are in fact going to have to find a way to bridge the gap between being a traditional networker and a guerrilla networker, because you may not be as far along as you would like.

For instance, you very well *may* appear at a party where absolutely no one knows who you are. Well, in this situation, you *still* must utilize guerrilla networking principles as best you can. You must — keyword: MUST — turn the tables as quickly as possible by actively and immediately taking steps to become the type of person other people at the party want to meet. For instance, if no one knows you at the party, and you're a great singer, and they suddenly announce karaoke — ta da! — you just solved the problem. While the traditional networkers would perhaps wait until the person they wanted to meet goes up and sings a song to approach and pitch this person, the guerrilla networkers would go up and sing themselves, and by doing so, perhaps encourage that other person to come up to them and congratulate *them*!

But by and large, your mission should be to try to avoid this. If at all possible, you want to already *be* the Guerrilla, and let the other person — from the get-go — be the traditional networker. The reason is simple: it puts you in the power seat. Arriving as the Guerrilla must be your number one networking priority — even if it takes 1, 3, or 10 years to become that person. Always and continually ask yourself, "What can I do today — at this very moment — that is going to make me the life of the party tomorrow? What can I do today that is going to make me be the type of person other people want to meet tomorrow? Next week? Next month? Next year?"

Please understand — this principle does not just apply to parties. It applies to life. In all cases and in all situations, you want your reputation to precede you. You want others to want to meet you. It has nothing directly to do with 'parties'; that is just the example we have chosen to use in this context. When we say 'party', we mean 'life'. And we want you to be the life of the party, and to live one wild party of a life.

That being said, in many ways, the easiest way to differentiate traditional networking tactics from those of the guerrilla is as follows: Traditional networking focuses on 'going to the party'. Guerrilla networking tactics focus on 'getting that party to come to you'.

This is why guerrilla networking is far more profitable in the long-term than traditional networking. Think how much money you would save if — instead of having to continually go out to 'parties' to find business — those very people brought that business (and the party) to you? Gosh, it just makes such total sense now doesn't it?

Although guerrilla networking requires that you work harder on the front end (by constantly developing and investing in yourself), in the final analysis, it is this strategy that has resulted in all of the great success stories in history. Those people who have succeeded on any great scale all have one thing in common: they became so successful precisely because they took the time to become the type of person other people wanted to meet (and we'll discuss some of these tactics in depth in Part II, and show you how to create your very own strategy in Part IV.)

Note that it is *not* the other way around. History's success stories did not typically first become successful and then, as a result, become the type of person other people wanted to meet. No. The Guerrilla mentality came first; then the success. The desirability came first, and then the success. And when you think about that, it makes perfect logical sense.

All of the great successful people in history all had one thing in common, and did that one thing very well, and consistently. What was it? Consciously or not, these people focused on — can you guess? — becoming the type of person other people wanted to meet. They did not go out trying to meet people. Edison did not focus on finding someone to buy his unfinished light bulb. No, he worked on it alone failing hundreds and hundreds of times until he made a *successful* light bulb (and thus truly became the type of person others wanted to meet). The Wright Brothers did not focus on trying to find people to buy their blueprints for an airplane. No, they built it themselves and even risked their lives flying it (and thus truly became the type of person others wanted to meet). Martin Luther King, Jr. did not focus on complaining privately about the plight of his people. No, he took a stand and publicly — and bravely — began the civil rights movement in earnest (and as a result, truly became the type of person others wanted to meet.)

These examples are unlimited. And telling. Networking success is not about meeting people. It sounds so counter-intuitive, we know. Yet it is the truth.

Consider this: if you start off with two equally competitive people and one of them focuses for 10 years on 'meeting people' and the other on 'becoming the type of person others want to meet', it's a no brainer who is going to be more successful in the end. The Guerrilla. Every single time.

CHAPTER 4:
Six Degrees & the Name Game

Truth be told, guerrilla networking is extremely rare. How do we know this? Well, most of the people in the world do not appear to be that interesting. To many readers, that might seem harsh, but realize we did not say that they are uninteresting; just that they appear so.

In other words, guerrilla networking is more than just becoming the type of person others want to meet. It is also about letting others know that you are the type of person others want to meet.

Yes, ladies and gentlemen, it is your responsibility to ensure that your client base, customer base, and fan base know that you are someone they should want to — and in fact — NEED to meet.

Guerrilla networking is essentially then a two-step process:

1) doing whatever is necessary to become the type of person other people want to meet and then;

2) making sure that everyone knows it.

If you skip either step... you are not going to see much success. If you satisfy step 1, but skip step 2, you may indeed be amazing, but no one will know it. On the other hand, if you skip step 1, and jump to step 2, everyone may know you, but not as someone they want to work with. It's a two step process, and it is your responsibility to make sure that you adhere to and follow each step. Ignore these imprecations at your own risk, and at the peril of your business success. As you may have noticed, the networking strategies of most people seem to skip one or both of those steps.

You see, most people never even realize that their 'lack of success' problem has little do with who they don't know, but rather with how poorly they are approaching the people they already know. In fact, we even believe that you already know everyone you need to know in order to be successful. Right now, you have every contact you need in order to make your business and life dreams come true... if only you would change your sales pitch, and in most cases, just make the pitch in the first place!

I call this my one-degree networking philosophy. I believe that right now, you already know all the people you need to know in order to take your life, career, and business where you want it to go. Forget six degrees! You don't need to go that far! Six may not seem like a lot of degrees, but it actually is. That's why it's foolish to even consider the notion that you are that far away from your dream contacts: you see, if you think you are six degrees away from the people you need to meet... then you are going to become overwhelmed!

You *already* know the people who can connect you to those you want to meet, and in fact, right now, at this very moment, you are only one degree (not six) away from everyone you need to meet.

The key is getting these people to want to help you, and making it abundantly clear how they can be of assistance.

For example, let's assume that you are planning to take an ad out in *Entrepreneur Magazine*. You've known your friend Bill for years, and he has always been helpful in providing advice to you to help with your business. Here are two potential scripts:

SCRIPT ONE

BILL: So, what's the latest?

YOU: I'm chugging along with my business. Working on some new advertising initiatives.

BILL: That's great. What exactly?

YOU: Working on some ads. Not really sure yet. I'll let you know when I figure it all out.

SCRIPT TWO

BILL: So, what's the latest?

YOU: I'm chugging along with my business, working on putting together a half-page ad for *Entrepreneur Magazine*.

BILL: *Entrepreneur*, huh? Ya know, you just reminded me. A friend from college just emailed me last week. He's actually an editor at *Entrepreneur* right now. Maybe instead of an ad, I can help you get a full story.

YOU: No way, Bill! Are you serious?! That would be amazing!

So, what was the difference? Why was there such a different result even though the characters in this script were the same?

The answer is simple: you gave the right pitch. You said the right words. You were clear and specific and focused and ambitious... and you shared that ambition with the world.

You see, the more focused & ambitious you appear, the more confidence you exude. The more confidence you exude, the more likely others will come to your aid, because everyone wants to help a winner. Especially a winner who just happens to be an underdog.

The key here is that your friend, Bill, has selective memory, just like all of us. Unless something triggers that specific memory, it remains buried under mounds of daily stress, advertising messages, and to-do lists. So, it's your job to help jog that selective memory.

In both scripts, Bill knew that editor at *Entrepreneur*. The difference? In the second script, you triggered his selective memory, and brought to his attention the email he had received last week. He knew all along that he knew this guy, but there was no memory trigger between his friend and you... until you said the right words: taking an ad out in *Entrepreneur*.

As soon as you became the type of person that the editor of *Entrepreneur* wanted to meet... you hit paydirt. And your friend — who you wrongly assumed didn't 'know' anyone who could help you — actually turns out to be your best resource.

The bottom line is that you truly do already know everyone you need to know in order to make your dreams come true. Often the difference between finding the 'connection' and not, is just a matter of saying the right words at the right time in the right way *to the people you already know.*

Most people try for years to 'meet people' with shamefully poor results in terms of their bottom line. They waste years — desperately and ultimately unsuccessfully — trying to push their way into offices, into parties, and into people's lives. It's rude, uncouth, and at the end of the day, a waste of time: not only haven't you met anyone, but you haven't changed, developed, or improved in any way as a person. You were so focused on meeting people that you completely neglected the number one focus of guerrilla networking: a focus — not on meeting people, but on becoming the type of person other people want to meet.

The good news is that you can kill two birds with one stone by becoming a guerrilla networker. Guerrillas expand their business & personal network while at the same time improving themselves and their business. And that is the focus of the next chapter.

But before we move on, we want to share with you something rather intriguing. Monroe pointed out to me (Jay) that 'if people don't remember your name, it's your fault.' What he means is that if someone doesn't remember your name, it's precisely because you obviously are not all that memorable! Or at the very least, you are not sharing your 'memorability' with people in a very effective way.

The next time you are at a party, a function, or even on a sales call, think about this concept. If people don't remember your name, it's your fault.

Take note: this one oft-overlooked principle is one of the hubs of 'guerrilla networking', and applies to every aspect of all you do in life, business, and everything in between.

CHAPTER 5:
How To Become Desirable
(i.e. the type of person other people want to meet)

Far too many people believe that popularity leads to desirability, but fortunately, it's the other way around. Desirability leads to popularity. This is fortunate because popularity is not something you can actually control very easily, but desirability is — and becoming desirable is the whole point of this book.

I often ask people to consider the question, "How Cool Are YOU?" The whole idea is that there is — in my opinion — an actual progression towards popularity that many are not aware of:

Uniqueness ➤ Coolness ➤ Desirability ➤ Popularity

If you focus on the last quality (popularity)... you won't get it. Popularity is something that others bestow upon you. Therefore, you can't control it. In fact, even desirability, which is a quality that can be influenced in a more concrete way is still not as controllable as the first two qualities: your coolness and your uniqueness. And go figure, your coolness is a direct reflection of how unique you and your company are. And if we're talking about being unique, we are talking about being different, and we're now back at the 1st book in the Guerrilla series: *Guerrilla Marketing*.

So focus — not on being popular — but instead on being unique. If you are truly unique (and use guerrilla marketing principles to let everyone know) success is going to find you.

Which leads us to the idea of network hubs. If you've read any other books on networking and persuasion, you have certainly come across this topic.

Basically, a network hub is someone who has access to exponentially more people and/or is exponentially more influential than a random 'joe' off the street. Examples of network hubs are people like Oprah Winfrey, companies like Microsoft, and on a smaller but similar scale, the president of a school's student union.

Well, your mission as a guerrilla networker is twofold: a) you want to entice as many network hubs as possible to meet you (notice we didn't recommend that you necessarily should try to meet them), and b) you want to do everything within your power to become a network hub yourself. The beauty of this approach is that by doing (b), you inevitably end up accomplishing (a). Think about that for a moment. By becoming a network hub yourself, you are going to naturally entice other network hubs to want to meet you.

Remember, if you are truly unique (in a good Tom Peters WOW type of way), and you tell the world, then people are GOING to want to meet you. It's a simple law of guerrilla networking. As a result of doing this, you are in essence becoming a network hub: the more people who want to meet you, the more influential you are becoming. Hint: if you haven't already, start keeping track of every single person you meet and also want to meet. The financial services industry uses an amazing index card based system (called the *One Card System*) that is simply amazing.

Developing the 'one-degree' concept further, now is a good time to also explain the difference between direct and indirect networks. Very simply, your direct network is everyone *you* know *who also knows you*, whereas your indirect network consists of all of the people who you are *related to* through your direct network, but who *don't currently know you*.

The truth of the matter is that if you simply focus a little more strongly on your *direct* network, you might quickly find that you are closer to the people you want to meet than you realize. Wouldn't it be nice to supercharge and wake up your indirect networks by turning the tables; by enticing your *indirect* network into finding *you* through mutual direct connections? Through the people you *already know*? That's one-degree networking.

The whole idea of guerrilla networking is to add a new dimension to traditional networking. Traditional networking is sometimes a very useful strategy, but it cannot be the only definition of networking that you rely on if you and your business hope to survive. Remember, guerrilla networking and traditional networking are two sides of the same coin.

For a business to succeed in this day and age, not only do you have to make efforts to meet people, but you have to also make great efforts to entice those very people into wanting to meet you. It's such an obvious concept once you think about it: if you don't know Keanu Reeves, and you want to meet him, what do you do? Do you spend every waking hour desperately 'trying to meet him' like a stalker? Or might it make more sense to say to yourself, "Hmmm, right now, Keanu doesn't know who I am and doesn't want to meet me. Three years are going to pass anyway. Instead of trying to desperately meet him, why don't I instead put more of my networking effort into becoming the type of person that he himself actually wants to meet!" It is simple logic, and it makes perfect sense. And three years later, you are more likely to have met him than by spinning wheels trying to meet *him*.

Let's play it out. You've decided to launch a guerrilla networking plan to meet Keanu. Let's say that you then do some analysis and conclude that Keanu would probably want to meet someone who:

a) can hire him as an actor

b) can offer him an amazing and fun acting role

c) can get him an interview on national television

In this case, who is this person that can provide these things? The answers are limitless: a millionaire who can finance one of his pet projects; an executive producer who can match his pet project to millionaires; a screenwriter who has a script written specifically for him; a news producer who works at one of the various cable or network news channels or talk shows; or even just someone who can introduce him to one of these people.

In fact, if we do even more research, we would discover that Keanu is from Hawaii. Hmmm... Perhaps he might have a soft spot for others from Hawaii.

Now, suddenly, you have myriad ways to entice Keanu into wanting to meet you. None of them are easy, but guerrilla networking is *not* easy; it's just simple. And like anything else, it does *become* easy if you are willing to work really really hard to make it that way.

Instead of desperately calling his agents and managers as a 'nobody', now, after doing the work to become the type of person he wants to meet, you can approach Keanu's agents and managers as a 'somebody'. Heck, he may have by now already called you!

Easy? No. But doable, YES! And you are virtually *guaranteed* that Keanu Reeves will want to meet you if you do the above things, and that should be pretty inspiring to you.

You might notice that what we did here is indeed combine both guerrilla networking *and* traditional networking. The first half of the equation was figuring out who exactly Keanu would want to meet... and doing everything in your power to become that person (guerrilla networking). The second half of the equation was to call his agents, managers, publicists, etc and let the world *know* that you are the type of person Keanu would want to meet (traditional networking).

The bottom line of this entire book is that you are sitting on a networking gold mine right at this very moment, if only you would open your eyes. As long as you are willing to take a long-term perspective on your life, career, and business; are not looking for a quick fix; and are obsessed enough to do the work necessary to become the type of person others want to meet... you are going to become *very* successful, and stay that way. *GUARANTEED.*

PART 2

50 Proven Ways to Get People to Come to You

TACTIC 1:
Write a Successful Book

You have heard this before. We know. We know that every other 'business book' you have read has encouraged you to write a successful book. We know that you are probably rolling your eyes already at the suggestion.

Consider this, though. Do you — the reader — personally know either Monroe or Jay? If you *do* know us, doesn't it make you feel proud to know us? Isn't the fact that the names Jay Conrad Levinson & Monroe Mann are listed on the front covers make us both more intriguing and interesting characters? If you *don't* personally know us, doesn't this book in your hands make you more likely to want to meet us?

The reason why so many others have recommended a book as a credibility builder is because it actually works. For some reason, if you have a book published with your name on the front cover as the author... it means you are accomplished; somebody of importance — it means you have something to say; that you are the expert; that you on top of your game; that you are worth meeting.

All of these perceptions combine together in the minds of a prospect creating a subconscious desire to want to meet you.

The reason why we list 'Write a successful book' as the first of our 50 proven ways to get people to come to you is because it is, quite frankly, easy. Both of us have written and published a number of successful books and as a result, people that we would never have come into contact with otherwise have become fans, friends, potential clients, and valued business partners. All simply because we are published authors.

If you are one of our many readers who *already* has a successful book published, our recommendation doesn't stray too far from the well: publish *another* successful book. Staying at the top of your field and in your prospect's mind requires constant attention and mainte-nance. You can never rest on your laurels. You need to always be one step ahead. Do it. Write another book. Right now. Make it even more successful than your last.

Remember this: the more often your name appears in print (no matter where), the more people are naturally going to want to meet you.

TRADITIONAL NETWORKING:
"Reading books by others who you one day hope to meet."

GUERRILLA NETWORKING:
"Writing books yourself that are going to entice others to want to meet you."

TACTIC 2:
Become the Expert in Your Field

Obviously, as we discussed on the previous page, by simply writing and publishing a book, you are going to inevitably earn respect as an expert in your field. But simply writing a book only makes you *an* expert; it doesn't make you *the* expert.

When you are *the* obvious expert (as Elsom and Mark Eldridge discuss in their book *The Obvious Expert*) — and people KNOW it — you will never have a problem getting people to want to meet you. In fact, the problem you are more likely to face is having to turn business away, decline requests to be interviewed, and pick and choose with whom you decide to spend your time. Frankly, that's a problem we know you all would be pleased to struggle through.

They are many ways to become known as the expert in your field. Yes, you need to write your book(s). You also need to offer something that no one else offers. You need to be the first person/business someone thinks of when they need your service. You need to be the best at what you do. You need to be more generous than others in giving away information at no charge. You need to have clients so enamored with your service and product that they blab about you to all of their friends. You need to be associated with other experts.

You need to be interviewed on a national television talk-show or news program. This list can and does go on and on.

The point is that when you become publicly known as the expert at what you do, word is going to spread. The very people who need your service/product are going to flock to you in droves if you are considered the expert. Everyone likes to be associated with an expert, if only for the prestige gained by doing so.

Now sure, becoming known as 'the expert' is no small feat. It potentially could take you months, or even years to get known as such. But if you are reading this book, it is safe to assume that you are on this entrepreneurial journey for the long haul, and that you have every desire to actually become this very expert. So who cares how long it takes? Do what needs to be done. Get started today.

While becoming known as the expert in your field may be a painful journey requiring lots of hard work, determination, blood, sweat, and tears... one day, you'll wake up and realize that you *are* that person you always wanted to be. You'll wake up and realize that you no longer have to search for prospects. Finally, after all this time, you will smile, sitting back by the pool, and listen as your cell phone rings nonstop. Finally, your prospects are searching for *you*.

TRADITIONAL NETWORKING:

"Trying to meet and become friends with the experts in your field."

GUERRILLA NETWORKING:

"Working to become one of those very experts yourself."

TACTIC 3:
Become Famous

This really isn't as far-fetched as you might think. There are many varying degrees of fame, and you may just need one or two to stand out. You can become famous in your community; famous in your company; or of course, famous internationally. Bottom line, you just want to become as famous as you possibly can be.

Now, why do you want to become famous? The answer is truly simple: people want to meet famous people. If you are famous, it means you are desirable, hot, in demand, on fire. If you are famous, there is going to be a line of people waiting to shake your hand and take you out to dinner... and that's the essence of guerrilla networking: becoming the type of person other people want to meet.

Keep in mind that if you are famous, it takes the networking burden off of your shoulders. Famous people are famous precisely because of the sheer volume of people who want to meet them. The logical question, then, is how to become famous...

Well, first off, a definition of being famous. At its core, it means that people know you well enough that your name now has clout. Even more simply, being famous just means that a large number of people know who you are. And that in itself is power. And if you're powerful, people will want to meet you.

Is it incredibly difficult to become famous? No, not *incredibly* difficult. To become famous in any capacity, it requires nothing more than simple appeal, on a large scale. Difficult, but simple. If you invent something, cure something, discover something, create something, deliver something, fix something, or receive something — something of value and importance — then the fame you seek will come as a matter of course.

Key point: first comes the contribution to society; then comes the fame. Don't focus on the fame; focus on the flame of contribution, and fuel it with everything you've got.

TRADITIONAL NETWORKING:
"Dreaming of meeting famous people."

GUERRILLA NETWORKING:
"Becoming a famous person so other famous people want to meet you."

TACTIC 4:
Offer Investment Capital

He who has the gold makes the rules. Or so the saying goes. Truth be told, if you can offer money for an entrepreneur's project... you are going to become one popular person. You are going to have so many people knocking on your door that you might regret having offered in the first place. Truly, if you put a classified ad in the newspaper that simply said, "Investor seeking projects, call...," you would have to set up a boiler room just to handle all of the incoming traffic.

As you may know if you have started your own business, trying to raise the seed and/or expansion capital can be painful and depressing. Given that, don't you see how many people would love to meet you if you were to become their saving grace; if you were to relieve some of the pain and provide some sunshine to their entrepreneurial exploits by giving them the money they need?

Once you start letting out that you are looking to invest in someone's project or business, your *personal* 'net worth' just went up through the roof. People are going to be introducing you to people; connecting you with people; and introducing themselves to you at every possible moment. Best part: in most cases, these are going to be some really cool, influential, and visionary people. People that you would benefit from meeting.

The best part is that by offering investment capital, you are going to benefit in more ways than just finding a potentially lucrative money maker to involve yourself with. Beyond it all, you are making a name for yourself as a really cool person. 'Cause folks, there are few people cooler in peoples' minds than the investors. If you are an investor, you are cool. There are no ifs, ands, or buts about it. He who provides the money is Mr. Cool.

TRADITIONAL NETWORKING:
"Trying to meet money people."

GUERRILLA NETWORKING:
"Offering to invest in other people's projects, thus becoming a money person yourself."

TACTIC 5:
Be a Network Hub

A network hub is a person with influence, clout, and a platform, i.e. someone that people go to and trust for advice. Guess what? You need to become that person.

You can become a network hub in a lot of ways, and some of you may already be a network hub. Ask yourself, "Do people ever come to me for advice?" "Do I ever speak or connect with an audience of greater than 10 people at one time?" "Am I a respected person in my business, field, or community?" If you answered 'yes' to any of those questions, then you are already on the road to becoming a large-scale network hub.

For those of you who are not yet at that point, take heart, you're not that far behind. There are so many simple and easy ways to become a network hub. A few examples are starting a blog online, starting a web-based radio station, teaching a class, writing a book, taking a stand on an issue and becoming the expert, and this list goes on. The key ingredient to becoming a network hub is to do something significant that people can rally behind. It doesn't need to be HUGE, just significant. Something that makes a difference.

The whole idea is to — through focused effort — become someone with influence, clout, and a platform. To become a network hub. The example used in many networking books is an airport.

How many different airports do YOU connect to? Are you a local airport that doesn't have any connections to major airports, or are you in fact one of those major airports, with connections to every other major airport? The larger an airport you are, the more planes (i.e. people) are going to want to land there. You need to do everything within your power to continue moving towards becoming one of those large airports.

There is no better way to radically expand your influence than by becoming a network hub yourself and having others come to you in search of YOUR approval. On the same note, nothing you ever do will get any publicity or reach any great level of success without first gaining the attention and support of other network hubs. You need to find out who these network hubs are, and then convince them that you and your projects are worthy of association. You need to become the type of person that network hubs want to meet and hang out with. This is a simple process: just follow the principles of guerrilla networking as presented in this book.

TRADITIONAL NETWORKING:
"Working to discover who the network hubs are and desperately trying to connect with them."

GUERRILLA NETWORKING:
"Becoming a network hub yourself so others want to connect with you."

TACTIC 6:
Get Media Exposure

As mentioned before, we have a fascination with famous people. For most of us, there is an aura of power and prestige bestowed upon those who are seen on television, heard on the radio, or read about in print. Beyond that, one of the simple formulas for getting people to want to meet you is simply letting others know what you are doing, and telling them why they should want to meet you. There is often no better way to do this than by being interviewed on a tv or radio show, by appearing as an actor on a tv or radio show, by being the host of a tv or radio show, by being mentioned on a tv or radio show, by being written up in an article, by getting an article of your own published, or — heck — even just being seen/mentioned in an advertisement.

The point is clear: Get onto TV. Get onto radio. Get into print. As soon as you possibly can. The sooner you do this and the more often you do this, the more quickly and forcefully people are going to want to meet you.

We've all heard someone justify something by saying, "I heard about it on the radio." Or I saw it on television. Or I read about it in the newspaper. There is a reason for this: there is respect and credibility associated with the media.

TRADITIONAL NETWORKING:
"Trying to get media attention."

GUERRILLA NETWORKING:
"Doing such cool things that the media are vying for your attention."

TACTIC 7:
Take Matters Into Your Own Hands

If you sit around hoping that the networking opportunities you are looking for are just going to magically appear of their own accord... you are gravely mistaken. The key to networking success is to take matters into your own hands.

In other words, get up out the door and make your own opportunities. There is an interesting correlation between the amount of opportunities you make for yourself and the amount of interesting people who want to meet you and shake your hand. No one wants to meet a 'nobody'; people want to meet and associate with a 'somebody', and that somebody is usually someone who took matters into his own hands.

So ask yourself, right now, what you might be able to do at this very moment — or in the next week, month or year — to take matters into your own hands. Why wait for someone else to create the opportunity for you? What can you do right now to set a chain of events into motion that puts the odds in your favor?

As physics makes clear, every action has an equal but opposite reaction. If you put forth effort, effort will put forth results. Never for a moment think that you have 'done enough'. You have not done enough until you are exactly where you want to be with your life. And the only way you are going to get exactly where you want to be with your life is to — you guessed it — take matters into your own hands.

People respect, honor, and look up to those who have a clear vision and purpose, and those who take the scary but necessary steps in order to make that vision and purpose a reality. If you hope to become the type of person others want to meet... find the guts to do what you need to do to get where you want to go. Everything else will just fall into place.

TRADITIONAL NETWORKING:
"Waiting for things to happen on the world's terms."

GUERRILLA NETWORKING:
"Making things happen on your terms."

TACTIC 8:
Offer to Help People

Send a check to the person you want to meet... made out to their favorite charity. Keep doing this in small amounts over and over with a new letter each time. Eventually, these people will want to meet you.

Few seem to understand that only by helping others and thinking of others can one ever reach great heights. Truly, what use is any fame or stardom or power if it isn't used for good?

Take some time to figure out how and why your success will help others, and then perhaps more people will reach out to help you get there. The reason why so many not-for-profit companies receive donations is because people feel good about helping those types of organizations. If you can make people feel the same way about helping you, you are going to receive more help immediately. And when you feel the same way about helping others, the circle of giving will be complete and all of your dreams will — like magic — start falling into place. You'll even feel better about your drive for success because it won't only be about you — when you succeed, hundreds of others will benefit as well.

TRADITIONAL NETWORKING:

"Trying to get everyone else to help you."

GUERRILLA NETWORKING:

"Offering to help someone else."

TACTIC 9:
Introduce Yourself to People

One of the easiest ways to get people to want to meet you... is by introducing yourself as someone worthy of being met. Sure, this is an outgrowth of traditional networking, and so be it. The fact remains that if you do this (introducing yourself) properly, everyone you meet is going to want to meet you too, and moreover, these people are going to want their friends to meet you too: "Hey Vanessa, you *gotta* meet this guy."

So stop being so nice. It's time to become more outgoing than you've even been in your life. So outgoing that some people don't even understand you and find you odd.

You need to get over any hesitation and doubt and self-consciousness and start introducing yourself to people. To everyone. To anyone. First and last name. Repeatedly. Proudly. With hand outstretched. In front of a group of strangers. At a private party. On cyberspace. In outerspace. In innerspace. Everywhere. Everyone.

For many people, talking about their accomplishments and ambitions makes them feel sick, nervous, or 'pushy'. However, to neglect this simple networking tool is potentially career suicide. Talk it up! Talk about why people should want to meet you.

You should be able to come up with a brief introduction that WOWs people into awe about you. It really shouldn't take much. Here are a few examples:

"Hi, I'm Monroe Mann, author of *The Theatrical Juggernaut*, CEO of Unstoppable Artists, and founder of the Juggernaut Club, the world's only inspirational networking action group for winners."

"Hi, I'm Jay Levinson, Father of *Guerrilla Marketing*, author of Guerrilla Marketing, and president of Guerrilla Marketing International."

"Hi, I'm John Doe, creator of the super widget."

"Hi, I'm Jane Da, founder of widget service."

"Hi, I'm Jonas Dodo, and I am going to be President of the United States in 8 years."

"Hi, I'm Janis Dada, and my new book is going to rocket to the top of the NY Times Best-Seller List."

You see, it's not that hard. You just need to start doing really cool things, and start telling people about them — in a clear and concise manner. Simple.

TRADITIONAL NETWORKING:
"People forgetting about you as soon as you leave."

GUERRILLA NETWORKING:
"Everyone talking about you long after you leave."

TACTIC 10:
Always Smile

Why does it seem like the world is depressed? I was walking down the streets of Moscow about 7 years ago, and it struck me so strongly when I realized that absolutely *no one* was smiling. No one. Everyone had these stoic, depressed, 'my life sucks' expressions on their face.

Yet, it hit me even more strongly when I realized that Moscow wasn't the only city afflicted. I see this everywhere. Even walking down the streets of Manhattan. Rarely do you see people smiling walking down the street. In the elevators: no smiles. In the offices: no smiles. In the delis: no smiles. No smiles!

Well, you are going to use this to your advantage. It is a proven fact that people want to hang out, work, and associate with winners and with happy people. The easiest way to come across as a winner... is by smiling. It is so simple, right? If so, then why do so few people do it? Why? Because it is *not* easy. It takes a lot of work to put a smile on your face when you don't feel like smiling constantly. But if you do, you'll notice a few things happening:

a) you'll actually feel happier immediately as a result of smiling;

b) you'll become more productive, because happy people work more efficiently;

c) you'll become more popular and desired, because you are giving off an inviting and welcoming vibe as a result of smiling;

d) others are going to smile back.

Just smile! Smile for no reason whatsoever. People are going to start talking to you simply because it is odd, asking, "Why are you smiling?" They want to know. They want whatever you have. They want to be like you. They want whatever 'you are on'. So get high on life, and start smiling. All the time. Right now. For the rest of the time you are reading this book... try smiling. Try smiling in random places. Smile when you are talking on the phone. Try smiling even when you are alone. Just with yourself. You'll find that you yourself become more proud of yourself just by simply smiling.

Are you smiling now? You should be. SMILE!!!

TRADITIONAL NETWORKING:
"Unconsciously seeking pity via your frowns."

GUERRILLA NETWORKING:
"Consciously attracting alliances with your smiles."

TACTIC 11:
Initiate Conversations

Yes, this simple act can get people to want to meet you. Most people are shy.

They are unclear about who they are, and where they want to be. So, it behooves you to pick up the slack.

In many cases, people *do* in fact want to meet you, but don't have the guts or the confidence to approach you themselves. In many cases, you need to be the person who bridges the gap for them.

Does this contradict our definition of networking? Not at all. As was mentioned, sometimes you have to use elements of traditional networking in order to get guerrilla networking to work best to your advantage.

You see, you are still becoming the type of person they want to meet by simply approaching them and saying the right things. A-ha! Did you read that? It's more than just approaching them; you also have to say the right things. You have to approach them and make them say things like, "Wow!" "No kidding!" "Yes, that is exactly the problem I am facing and I am so pleased to have run into you so you can help me solve it!"

So don't be hesitant to approach others. Don't be hesitant to take that chance. Don't be hesitant to send that email. Heck, that's how

I ended up meeting and becoming friends with Jay in the first place: I initiated a conversation with him. He then decided I was someone that he wanted to meet, wrote me back, and that's all she wrote!

TRADITIONAL NETWORKING:
"Hoping that everyone already knows who you are."

GUERRILLA NETWORKING:
"Assuming no one does."

TACTIC 12:
Become 'Cool'

I t's a fact of life. People want to be around and hang out with the 'cool' people, whoever they may be.

So... become cool! Do cool things. Do things that entice people to constantly and continually call you 'cool'.

Do people call you cool now? If not, why do you think that is? Strive to change who you are so that you become 'cool' in others' eyes.

If people already do call you cool, ask yourself the same question? Why is this? And strive to magnify that coolness.

Take a good hard look at the people you currently want to meet and ask yourself, "Why is this person cool? Why do I want to meet this person?" Whatever answers you get, see if you can emulate that coolness in your own self and in your own business.

I hope it is apparent to you that when we say 'cool', we mean what is currently en vogue, what makes people say 'Wow!' — what excites people. It is not as superficial as it first may appear. It is what drives success! People buy what is cool! People wear what is cool! People do what is cool! Being cool is the cool thing to do!

Ask yourself, "How cool am I?"

TRADITIONAL NETWORKING:

"Trying to hang out with the 'cool' people."

GUERRILLA NETWORKING:

"Becoming that cool person yourself."

TACTIC 13:
Become Noteworthy

Do you understand what it means to be noteworthy? It means, go figure, "Worthy of Note." You might notice that noteworthy is closely related to its cousin, remarkable, which means, "Worthy of Remark."

Are you currently worthy of note and worthy of remark? On how large of a scale? If so, why are you noteworthy? What have you done to become worthy of note?

What can you do to become even more noteworthy?

Realize that becoming noteworthy requires that you *do something worthy of note*. So, the solution here is quite simple. Do something worthy of note, and voila, you too will become noteworthy. And when you become noteworthy, you will be duly noted! People will want to comment on your accomplishments. People will want... to meet you!

Right now, you are certainly not doing nearly as many noteworthy things as you should be doing... and you know this. Right now, there are a number of things you know you could be doing to stand out from the crowd; to make a mark for yourself... that you are not currently doing. Our advice is simple: do these things! Do the things that are going to set you apart from your competition. Do the things that are going to make you noteworthy.

If you take the time to do so, you'll quickly discover that you don't have to spend nearly as much time trying to meet people; they'll all be trying to meet you.

TRADITIONAL NETWORKING:
"Trying to connect with noteworthy people."

GUERRILLA NETWORKING:
"Becoming that noteworthy person yourself."

TACTIC 14:
Do Something Radical

o something radical? Yes! Yes! Do something radical. Do something crazy. Do something that is going to get you onto the front page news. Do something wild that is going to get your name buzzing in all the circles you want to be buzzing in. Do whatever it takes to get the attention of the people that you want to meet!

Obviously, you need to evaluate the potential backlash from any rebellious actions you decide to take, but rebellious action has historically resulted in most of the great stories in history, most notably the American Revolution. You need to be a little crazy, and your actions need to have a bit of a misfit quality to them in order to be noticed. No one who is 'normal' gets noticed. Only the change-makers, the crazy-makers, and the trend-setters get any credit or play.

So don't be afraid to be a little different, and a little psychotic even. Do something that makes people raise their eye-brows. Do something that gives people cause for pause. Do something that gets EVERYONE to know who the heck you are.

Now, what type of people would want to meet someone like this? The answer: lots of them. Just look around. The coolest companies and the coolest people are *not* normal by any stretch of the imagination. They are all doing things differently, uniquely, and questioning the status quo at every opportunity. Strive to be like these people and companies and you too will find that the coolest people will also want to meet, work, and hang out with you.

TRADITIONAL NETWORKING:
"Playing it safe."

GUERRILLA NETWORKING:
"Understanding that breaking the rules often reaps rewards."

TACTIC 15:
Become the Go-Between

This tactic is a true winner, and one that too many people ignore simply because their ego is too great.

In a nutshell: if you know prominent, successful, or influential people, and you don't let others know that you are in a position to potentially act as a go-between... you are truly limiting your networking potential.

Do you really want to be the person that others want to meet? It's simple: become a go-between! In other words, become a match-maker. Become that network hub we talked about earlier. Become the person that everyone knows is connected to everybody. Or even just connected to somebody. It doesn't matter as long as you are able to connect person A with person B. How do you benefit? By strengthening the relationship that you have with *both* of them! And by the fact that becoming known as this 'go-between' type of person, you will inevitably attract others who are similarly interested in being connected with your associates.

Now, of course, you don't just let anyone benefit from your connections. No, you obviously have to conduct a screening process of sorts, and this is easily accomplished: whomever wants to be connected through your network must first pitch their idea to you.

If you like it, and think your other connection would benefit, you make the match. Simple.

The biggest criticism of this technique is that people are fearful that if they become a go-between, then they will become *known* as a mere go-between, and not be recognized for their own unique talents and contributions. They also fear that they will be 'used' merely for their connections.

Folks, the only person who can allow you to be used is yourself, and frankly, to be known as a go-between in our book is a compliment you should not so quickly dismiss. Your own originality and uniqueness will certainly still shine through, and in the end, you'll benefit because now you have all of these amazing connections that you can now use for *your* own benefit.

TRADITIONAL NETWORKING:
"Assuming that being a go-between is an unsavory position to avoid at all costs."

GUERRILLA NETWORKING:
"Realizing just the opposite."

TACTIC 16:
Risk Failure

The world loves a great risk taker. Especially when he succeeds. But heck, even when he fails!

The reason this is so is because it takes guts to go out on a limb. It takes guts to try those things that most are too afraid to even consider.

The truth is that people like to hang out with winners. People like to hang out with people who take risks. It's fun! It makes their *own* life more exciting.

Beyond that... the only way you are going to become the type of person others want to meet is by becoming successful in some capacity. Success — as many of us know — is a direct result of failure. The more often we fail, the more opportunities we are giving ourselves to succeed. And the more we succeed, the inevitable result is the creation of desire in other people to want to meet you *because everyone wants to be friends with a winner.*

So the key here is to look far into the future and realize that the only way you are going to become successful on a large scale is to fall flat on your face as often as possible. Sounds illogical, but the truth of the matter is that this strategy may truly be the best advice we can give you if you really want to become the person or company that everyone wants to work with.

Remember, networking is about meeting people. Guerrilla networking is about becoming the type of person other people want to meet. By risking failure, you are — even it may not seem like it at the time — planting the very seeds for just such a networking bloom.

Think of the people who are most talked about: George Bush and his risks with the war; David Blaine and his risks with stunts; Jay Leno, David Letterman, Conan O'Brian, and Craig Ferguson and their risks every night as they get up to do their monologues before hundreds of millions of people. Gwen Stefani and her leaving *No Doubt*. And Jay Levinson and his risk working with me, Monroe Mann. These people are all taking risks every day of their lives. And the result is two-fold:

a) they end up accomplishing more than most people;

b) they as a result become the type of person that other people want to meet

We all love to be around people who are involved with great things, and who are every day striving to accomplish the impossible. It makes us too feel that we are great: just being in the company of greatness can make all of us feel spectacular.

So, become that person for someone else. Become great so that others too can feel great by being in your company. And how do you become great? By taking big risks.

TRADITIONAL NETWORKING:

"Avoiding risk."

GUERRILLA NETWORKING:

"Realizing that being 'risky' is often cool."

TACTIC 17:
Send Off an Email

As you read in the introduction, Jay & I truly made our first connection via email. This is the power of guerrilla networking working in reverse. You don't have to wait for someone else to contact you to be a practitioner of guerrilla networking. Not at all.

On the contrary, guerrilla networking often works best in reverse. In other words, *you* initiate the contact, but in the first few moments of the contact, you manage to say and do the right things so that you become the type of person your contact wants to meet. As an example, I sent Jay an email that contained text that convinced Jay that I was the type of person he would want to meet.

You can similarly do the same thing. Make sure that everything about every email you send off would make someone want to meet you. Do you have an eye-catching and clearly focused marketing angle in your signature line? Do you even use a signature line? Does it include your website and briefly explain why you are 'cool'? Does it make people say, "Wow"?

Every email sent off has the ability to get a response. You can get *anyone* to respond to your emails if only you said the right things in those emails. Don't think of it as 'just an email'. Instead, think of each email as your ticket to networking success; your admission fee to the millionaire's circle; your success blueprint. Each email can be worth hundreds of thousands of dollars if you would just look at each one from this new point of view and then take the time when crafting each email to ensure maximum guerrilla networking potential.

Before you send off each email, ask yourself, "Is there enough enticing information in this email to encourage the recipient to respond; is there enough information to make it clear that it is in fact in the recipient's best interest to respond?"

TRADITIONAL NETWORKING:
"Assuming you'll never get a response."

GUERRILLA NETWORKING:
"Realizing that you never know!"

TACTIC 18:
Be Creative

Truth be told, most people get nowhere with their networking initiatives simply because they lack creativity. As Jay points out in *Guerrilla Marketing*, creativity is simply the opposite of mediocrity. In other words... if you are creative, you are far more likely to stand out. And those that stand out are far more likely to pique the interest of others. Hence, the purpose of this book: piquing the interest of others so that they end up wanting to meet you.

To many people, being truly creative seems like a lot of hard work. Actually, if you just be yourself and take your wild ideas and run with them... you just might discover how truly creative you are. You see, we *all* are creative... at first. But when you are constantly told that your ideas are worthless, and that you 'shouldn't quit your day job', it tends to blow out the fire within us. We're here to tell you to get over all that... and be creative once again. Think big! Think outrageous.

Go back through your entire life and think of all the 'creative' ideas you came up with that people criticized. Bring them out of the closet. Dust them off, and get that creative engine running again. Again, as Jay points out in *Guerrilla Marketing*, creativity is simply the opposite of mediocrity. Being creative, then, is simply another way of saying, "Be original!" Be spontaneous. Be wild. Be crazy. Be anything but normal!

Normal equals boring. You can't do things the way everyone else does if you hope to stand out. And the only way anyone is going to want to hang out with you is if you stand out in some notable (which usually translates to creatively different) way!

TRADITIONAL NETWORKING:
"Believing that creativity is too hard."

GUERRILLA NETWORKING:
"Understanding that creativity is simply the opposite of mediocrity."

TACTIC 19:
Write a Spicy Letter to the Editor

Yes, writing a spicy — i.e. controversial — letter to the editor of a newspaper or magazine is sure to create some sensation. Pop your name and email address down in there as well, and you just might be meeting a lot more people than you know what to do with.

The idea is to create a controversy because of something you say. If you say something radical, only two things can potentially happen:

a) you are going to receive emails and phone calls from people who want to meet you because they agree with everything you just wrote about

b) you are going to receive emails and phone calls from people who want to meet you because they oppose everything you just wrote about

Either way, don't you see, *you win!* You win because you have accomplished exactly what guerrilla networking sets out to accomplish: attracting the very people you want to meet.

Sure, one might argue that you don't want to attract those who disagree with you, but that's not taking the bird's eye view. You see, first off, publicity is publicity. If people are talking about you, it means you are networking. It doesn't matter what they are talking about in particular — if they are talking about you, and want to meet you (for whatever reason), you are at least on the right track. More importantly, those that vocally disagree with you are doing you a favor: they are giving you the opportunity to change their minds. They obviously care enough to be vocal, and that says a lot, and you should take that strongly into consideration.

For the record, the 'spicy controversy' strategy discussed here can be applied to anything. It applies to public speaking, to teaching, to your marketing, to your press releases, to your advertising, and on and on. Be spicy with all that you do, and you'll end up with both fans and foes knocking at your door... and that's exactly the way you should want it to be.

TRADITIONAL NETWORKING:
"Playing it safe."

GUERRILLA NETWORKING:
"Creating a controversy."

TACTIC 20:
Write a Press Release

If you are reading this book, then you have probably read a number of other books in the Guerrilla series. If so, then you have probably read about press releases ad nauseum. And you are probably yawning right now. The idea of the press release is admittedly a very simple concept. So simple, though, that most people don't actually do it.

Here's the big ol' clincher: instead of yawning, why don't you write a press release? Right now. If the statistics hold true, the odds are that you probably haven't written a press release in the last six months. It's a wild and eye-opening reality: everyone nods their heads in agreement that press releases are one of the best ways of securing publicity... and yet so few people actually get off their butts and actually write them, let alone disseminate them to the media.

Quick tip: you want people to come to you and meet you, right? Well, as we discussed, you sometimes have to take that first step. That first step can be through a press release.

Guerrilla networking's premise is that you shouldn't be putting as much effort into meeting people as you should into enticing them to want to meet you. The good ol' fashioned press release is *exactly* meant for this very purpose. Instead of trying to meet every single person in New York City, for example, you simple entice the newspaper or magazine into wanting to meet you (through a press release) and then the newspaper or magazine then works to make the denizens of New York want to meet you.

One of the keys to effective marketing is consistency. A press release may be simple, but so simple that many people forget how powerful it actually is, and can be. Be consistent with press releases and the whole world could very shortly be knocking on your front door.

TRADITIONAL NETWORKING:
"Trying to actually meet the editors."

GUERRILLA NETWORKING:
"Enticing them into wanting to meet you."

TACTIC 21:
Hire a Publicist

What a novel idea, huh? If you want to become the type of person that others want to meet, then that sort of implies that others know who you are. Hiring a publicist is potentially one of the best ways to let others know who you are, why you are different, and what you have to offer the nation, and the world.

It's also one of the more expensive tactics as well, so you might want to also go back and read tactic # 20 (write a press release) before committing to this. However, the potential effectiveness of hiring a publicist cannot be understated. If you already *are* the type of person other people want to meet, then in many cases, all you simply need is exposure. A publicist may be able to help provide this exposure.

Another benefit of hiring a publicist is that the act itself is a reason for people to want to talk to you. Those people who have publicists typically *have something going on*. They typically are better than average, more than the expected, and different from the norm. Few people hire a publicist unless they have a unique life story providing ammunition to the publicist's arsenal. If you're at a party and mention, "Oh, well my publicist said," the next question very well may be, "Oh, why do you have a publicist?" Or if you say, "I just hired a publicist the other day," again, the logical anticipated response will likely be, "Oh really? Why?"

And now they just opened the door for you to talk about everything you are doing. How convenient.

Of course, hiring a publicist in and of itself is not going to create a path of people knocking on your door. But thinking in this publicist mentality just may. People who hire publicists generally have something wild, crazy, and interesting going on in their lives. You need to start thinking towards that end *now*.

With everything you do, ask yourself, "Would this interest people? Is what I am doing (or not doing) newsworthy? What can I do to make this of interest to the entire city/state/country/world?"

The answers to these questions will guide your guerrilla networking campaign.

TRADITIONAL NETWORKING:
"Doing it all yourself."

GUERRILLA NETWORKING:
"Using your limited time as effectively as possible."

TACTIC 22:
Find Their 'Sweet Spot'

Yes, it is true: EVERYTHING is negotiable. You see, whether people care to admit it, the truth is that everyone has a soft spot, a sweet spot, a magic spot... whatever you want to call it. This sweet spot turns other people to mush, and putty in your hands.

For me, my sweet spots are those who speak French, Italian, or Portuguese as their native tongue, and also, anyone who has ever served in the military. In other words, if you speak French, Italian, or Portuguese, or have ever served in the military (especially in combat), then you automatically get one up in my book. You automatically get 10 minutes of my time. You automatically are given preference over others who have *not* found my sweet spot.

The sweet spots change, obviously, person to person. One person may have a weakness for freshly made Swiss chocolate. Another may be head over heels for skiing. Another may be a member of a certain fraternity.

The point here is that if you want others to want to meet *you*, the easiest way for that to happen is to discover their sweet spots, and see if you can satisfy them. Or, go on an all-out search specifically to find people who have sweet spots that you know you can satisfy. Make sense? If you speak fluent Chinese, and are an ace computer programmer... then one of your missions should be seeking out those influential people who love Chinese and who enjoy talking about computer programming.

This sweet spot concept applies to all people, all projects, and all companies. There is no exception to this rule. The only caveat is that you have to be sure that you nail the right sweet spot. If you do, then this technique will work every single time.

In fact, this is the best negotiation tool out there. It is well worth your time to cultivate it to as much perfection as you can. If you start to have a sixth sense for sweet spots in other people, projects, and companies — if you start to know instinctively what others want — and you can provide them with it and help them realize that sweet spot, then you just jumped 10 miles ahead of the competition.

TRADITIONAL NETWORKING:
"Researching the person."

GUERRILLA NETWORKING:
"Understanding the person."

TACTIC 23:
Take Out an Ad

Again, guerrilla networking is not about meeting people, but instead, becoming the type of person other people want to meet. Simple. Straight forward. Case closed.

So, taking out an ad could certainly help you in that regard. And think big! What is some wild and crazy ad campaign that you could kick off, and preferably without spending too much money; something outrageous that would entice others to meet you? What could you say or do in that ad to make people think to themselves, "Wow, I want to meet that person?" If after seeing your ad, people are thinking anything *but* that, then there is a big problem with your ad campaign.

Remember, everything and anything you do should be aimed with the focus of enticing other people to want to meet you (and use your company's products and services.) If your advertisement does that... then you are guerrilla networking like a pro. However, if you are taking out ads and are not receiving the anticipated response... then it's the exact opposite: you are not espousing the principles of guerrilla networking. For remember, if done right, guerrilla networking encourages the very people you want to meet to *come to you*. It's all simply a matter of technique.

Whenever you take out an ad, always ask yourself, "Would I want to meet the person behind this advertisement and behind this company?" If the answer is 'no', then go back to the drawing board and come up with a new ad. Do *not* spend any of your advertising budget unless you are certain that the ad itself will entice the very people reading it to want to meet you.

TRADITIONAL NETWORKING:
"Going to the prospect."

GUERRILLA NETWORKING:
"Encouraging the prospect to come to you."

TACTIC 24:
Call Them

It confuses us greatly how few people have the guts to pick up the phone and *talk to someone*. Cold calling seems to be one of the most difficult endeavors for many people.

Here's the rub: what's the big deal? They're human, just like you! If you want to be a top-notch Guerrilla Networker, then you need people to know your name, and what you stand for, and perhaps most importantly, what you want! One of the best ways of doing this is by just picking up the phone and calling!

The key to getting over the jitters in most cases is simply having a sales script. Type it out. Print it out. Have it in front of you when you call. Make sure there are enough 'guerrilla networking' touch-points in the short pitch to get the attention of whomever it is you are speaking with.

Remember: be confident! Be confident that you are someone who they would want to meet... and then be sure to back it up with what you say. They may not know your name when they pick up the phone, but after 30 seconds, *they had better!* And they had better think *very highly* of that name.

Is it difficult to accomplish something like this in 30 seconds? Of course it is! It is also one of the best ways of convincing others that you are someone they should meet.

TRADITIONAL NETWORKING:
"Doing the bare minimum."

GUERRILLA NETWORKING:
"Doing whatever is necessary to make it happen."

TACTIC 25:
Leave a Voicemail

Yes, leave a voicemail. But a *good* voicemail. A voicemail that *sells*. It's a really simple procedure:

a) Figure out exactly what you want from the person

b) Write out a killer sales pitch, no longer than 30 seconds. Actually write it out. Practice it a few times. Make sure it gives them enough reason to 'want to meet you', i.e. call you back.

c) Make the call after hours when you know that the voicemail system will pick up.

This actually works. And for a variety of reasons:

a) You are less stressed because you are talking to a voicemail.

b) You do not have to 'get through' any secretaries or gatekeepers; you can start your pitch from the get-go.

c) You are giving them a great pitch but not wasting their time during the day.

To some, this might seem like a 'cop-out', as if the caller were too scared to call during the day, but that couldn't be farther from the truth. If you have a good pitch, it will very likely be *more* effective than if you had called directly.

Never forget the essence of guerrilla networking: with everything and anything you do — including leaving voicemails — you need to give the other party a reason to care. Here's a wake up call to many of you: if people are not returning your phone calls, you are the reason why. If your calls aren't being returned, it should be obvious that your message, your business, your name, or your pitch is just not urgent, pressing, or important enough for the other party to care. If so, your guerrilla networking campaign is failing, and in a very big way.

Ask yourself, "Are my phone calls returned promptly?" If so, figure out why, and do more of it. If not, figure out why not, and fix it. And if some of your calls are returned quickly, and some are not — which is probably the case with most people — who is it that is returning your calls quickly, and why are they doing that? And who is not returning your calls quickly, and why are they ignoring you?

The more you ask — and answer — these questions, the more successful a guerrilla networker you will become.

TRADITIONAL NETWORKING:
"Insisting on speaking with someone."

GUERRILLA NETWORKING:
"Ensuring that they call you back."

TACTIC 26:
Include Them in Your Acknowledgments

This technique, of course, implies that you are writing a book. Of course, we are blatantly hinting that you *should* be writing a book. Mentioning people in the acknowledgements to your book, you see, is perhaps one of the finest ways of letting someone know that you admire them, and appreciate them in some way. Putting someone else's name in print in a bound book that is sold publicly can make that person feel like a million bucks. In turn, that action often has the effect of making these people want to meet you.

I mentioned Jay in the acknowledgements to my first book, *The Theatrical Juggernaut,* and then sent him a copy. Who would've thunk that a few years later, I would be co-writing a book with him. That, in a nutshell, is the power of including someone in your acknowledgements. Were it not for me including him in the acknowledgements, I very well may never have sent him a copy of the book, and had I never sent him a copy of the book, then you very well might not be reading this one today.

So have fun with your acknowledgements! Make it a 10-page list of acknowledgements if you want. The more people you mention, the more likely some of these people are going to end up wanting to meet you.

Take note: you can acknowledge people in more places than just the front of a book. You can acknowledge people in public, at a banquet, during a meeting, in a memo, in an email.

This is so easy to do, and yet, so few people do it. Why not? If you publicly acknowledge people who have helped you and/or have been an inspiration to you — ya might be surprised — they might hear about it, and want to meet you.

Everyone likes and wants to feel important, and as those of us who have read *How to Win Friends & Influence People* know, when it comes to success in personal relationships, the key is in the *other* person, and not you. The same principles apply to guerrilla networking as well: it's not about you! It's not about you!

While the whole principle of guerrilla networking works only when you develop *yourself*, the whole point is that your development should be influenced by *other people*. In other words, follow your heart — yes — but as you do so, you should continually be trying to figure out what these other people might think is 'cool' as well.

To that end, it's a no brainer that most people would consider a public acknowledgement from you pretty cool in and of itself. So... be that person who publicly acknowledges others. If Oprah Winfrey mentions your name on her show, you're as good as golden. That is the power of public acknowledgement. If Oprah wants to meet someone, all she has to do is publicly acknowledge that person on her show, and you can be sure that person would find out about it in less than 24 hours. That is the power of public acknowledgement.

So who do you want to meet? Make your list. Now, publicly acknowledge each one! The more public the acknowledgement, of course, the more quickly this technique will work, but acknowledgement of any sort will usually eventually be passed along to the recipient. So start publicly acknowledging people for what they've done for you, and do this at every opportunity you can find!

TRADITIONAL NETWORKING:
"Yearning for the day when you are acknowledged by someone else."

GUERRILLA NETWORKING:
"Acknowledging the very people you seek acknowledgement from."

TACTIC 27:
Become Their Friend

You might not realize it, but most people in this world are lonely. As lonely as can be. Their life isn't what they hoped it would be, the people in it aren't who they dreamed they'd be hanging out with, and their problems seem to mount more and more each day. Gosh, most people would go to great lengths just to have a friend.

So, be a friend!

Too many people fail to approach people they want to meet because they come to the erroneous and self-conscious conclusion that the other person is too 'cool' or 'successful' to want to meet them. That couldn't be farther from the truth. We've all heard the expression, "It's lonely at the top," and well, it's true!

The more successful you become, the more difficult it is for other people to relate to you. As a result, they shy away from you, and not for lack of want, but for lack of confidence! These people would LOVE to meet you and talk to you, but hey, you haven't said anything to them!

In other words, be a friend! Get over your own 'lack of confidence' and approach them. Send them an email. Call them. Call their agent. Call their secretary. Write a letter. Acknowledge them publicly! Whatever you do, stop keeping it to yourself. You very well might be the very friend that this person is hoping to find, and the only way you'll seal the deal is by making the first move.

True, making that first move can be difficult, but nothing worth doing is easy. Find the guts to tell the people you admire how you feel. This world is a very strange place: you just may find that they admire you too.

TRADITIONAL NETWORKING:
"Wondering why you don't have more friends."

GUERRILLA NETWORKING:
"Working to become the type of person other people want to be friends with."

TACTIC 28:
Do Them a Favor

Want to get someone to want to meet you, or — in this case — feel obligated to meet you? Simply do them a favor!

Sure, no one 'asked' for the favor, but like it or not, if you do something for someone, there is a subconscious psychological desire and need to return the world into balance by returning the favor. If you can figure out what that other person wants, and give it to them without them asking for it, you may have just won a special place in their heart.

Step one, of course, is to determine who it is who want to meet. Step two is to determine what this person wants more than anything (but is having trouble finding). Then step three is to see what you can do to make that dream come true.

You of course need to be careful with this technique, because you don't want to come across as pushy or weird. And you certainly don't want to make it seem that you are only helping them for your own selfish interests: you truly do need to be helping them first and foremost because it will make their life easier or more enjoyable. If they then help you in return, that's a bonus.

Bottom line, it's all about finesse and charm. If you can dish out favors in a charming and charismatic manner, you win.

TRADITIONAL NETWORKING:

"Doing favors with an ulterior motive."

GUERRILLA NETWORKING:

"Doing favors with a generous motive."

TACTIC 29:
Let Them Do *You* a Favor

Now, this seems a bit backwards, right? Why would letting someone else do *you* a favor turn you into the type of person that they want to meet?

The answer is simple: too many people turn down favors from other people precisely because they don't want to feel obligated to that other person. And yet, that is precisely why you would want to let other people do favors for you.

You see, once you allow others to do favors for you, they will feel the subconscious necessity to stay in touch with you, in hope that the favor will be returned. More importantly, helping people makes others feel good. And when people feel good about themselves, they are generally more likely to help others. People like to feel powerful, and important, and those who are allowed to do someone else a favor often feel powerful and important.

If that all makes sense, you might be asking, "But how would someone I don't know ever be in a position to do me a favor?" The answer: because you force the cards. You navigate yourself into a position where they can help you, and want to help you. You are *not* manipulating them, but rather, are simply making it clear to this person that you can benefit from their help, and that you are welcome to receive it.

Again, too often, we seem to think that the successful people whom we admire don't have time for us 'little people', but the truth of the matter is that they would perhaps like nothing more than to be a mentor, and share some of the tips and tricks they have picked up over the years. A case in point here is me, Monroe Mann, who found a mentor in Jay Levinson. And in me, Jay Levinson, who found a protégé who I wanted to help out in Monroe Mann.

In this situation — as any guerrilla networking arrangement should be — we both win, and it's a win-win outcome for all involved. He helps me, and I help him. We both have something to gain from helping the other person, whatever it may be. For me, it's the knowledge, experience, and credibility I am gaining through working with Jay on this book. For Jay, it's the pleasure, satisfaction, and honor of helping out the next generation of guerrilla marketing masters.

TRADITIONAL NETWORKING:
"Not thinking highly enough of yourself."

GUERRILLA NETWORKING:
"Realizing that you deserve (and need) some help!"

TACTIC 30:
Say Thank You

No one thanks anyone anymore. It's disgusting. And rude. And arrogant. Just say thank you! Say thank you!

Say thank you to the postman.

Say thank you to your boss.

Say thank you to your employees.

Say thank you to your son or daughter's teacher.

Say thank you to someone who just made photocopies for you.

Say thank you to the person who just bought you lunch.

Say thank you to whomever puts up with your insanity on a daily basis.

Say thank you to your parents.

Say thank you to the guy who just ripped your movie ticket stub.

Say thank you to the woman who just served you.

Say thank you to the person who just spit in your face!

Just say thank you. Make it a habit to say thank you constantly, and you might start to realize that people are constantly regarding you more highly than ever before.

Take a moment to write a thank you note to every one of your clients. To every one who has ever sent you a gift. To every one who has helped you in some way.

Heck, in this day and age, even just sending a quick 10-second text message would be more appreciation than most people receive in an entire year.

If you truly want to become the type of person that others want to meet and work with... start saying thank you! ALL THE TIME! Just get over your own ego and sense of self-worth and start showing some appreciation for the work of others, and — wild notion — you might start to see that these same people start to show some appreciation for what you do, and begin making a more concerted effort to work with you.

Don't wait for others to show appreciation before showing yours. That is a backwards notion. SOMEONE has to set the ball in motion, and as a guerrilla, it should be you. Go ahead, and take the 'thank you' plunge. Once you start doing it, it'll become an addiction and a habit, and you'll start to wonder why you didn't start saying thank you sooner.

Oh, and lest you think you already say thank you often enough: YOU DON'T! Trust us. You don't. No one does. And that is the whole point.

TRADITIONAL NETWORKING:

"Hoping others will thank you."

GUERRILLA NETWORKING:

"Thanking them first."

TACTIC 31:
Become a Success in Your Field

There's a saying in show business (and probably many businesses): if you try to get signed to an agency, it'll never happen, but as soon as you become so successful that you don't need an agency, they all will want to sign you to their agency. Therefore, what's the best way to get an agent in showbusiness? Be so successful that you don't need one.

That advice is the same in any business, and is guerrilla networking in a nutshell: if you really want to meet a certain person, become so successful that they want to meet you. In other words, your mission must be to ensure that the tables are turned, i.e. that instead of them being in a position to help you, you become so successful that you are now in a position to help *them*. Once you can help someone more than they can help you, low-and-behold, you'll probably be getting a lot more phone calls from this person.

Although you may think that the only route to success is through a certain person or company... you are probably mistaken. Try to figure out all of the ways that you can accomplish your goals without 'meeting' these people, and then start moving forward. Once you do, it's amazing that suddenly those very people you 'needed' now want to jump on board your projects.

Yes, become a success in your field! *That* is going to get a lot of people to want to meet you. While it is true that in the beginning of the book we said that success is a by-product of guerrilla networking, it is also undeniable that once you do become a success, even more people are going to want to meet and work with you. And that's the point we are trying to make here.

TRADITIONAL NETWORKING:
"Believing success is 'the end.'"

GUERRILLA NETWORKING:
"Knowing success is part of 'the means.'"

TACTIC 32:
Help Someone Else Become Successful

We've all heard of the golden rule, namely that you should do unto others as you would have them do unto you. Well, there's a method to that madness. The more you help other people, the more other people will go out of their way to help you... including those very people who you want to meet.

If you take the time to think less of yourself, and more about other people, you will find that other people will also think less of themselves, and think more of you. They will then want to help *you* become more successful.

In other words, the more you help other people, the more you indirectly help yourself. What goes around comes around, and people *do* notice when you go out of your way to help someone else become successful.

You might be thinking, "But why would I want to meet someone who is not yet successful? Why would meeting this type of person help me in any way?" The answer is simple: With your help, this person could very well become successful, and in fact, might even become more successful than you. In this case, it should be clear that now this person that you helped is now in a position to help you. It's a simple case of you scratch my back, and I'll scratch yours.

Moreover, when other people see that you are helping someone get a leg up, they too may be similarly inspired to give someone a leg up. That 'someone' could very well be you. And the person giving the 'leg up' could very well be that very person you had hoped to meet, or someone you don't even know who is actually in a position to help you.

That is a key point worth mentioning: many times, you don't *know* who it is that you want to know. Often, that person is a good friend of yours and you didn't even know that he or she was in a position to help you out; heck, you just thought he was a monk, but alas, what you never knew is that he used to be a Navy fighter pilot and knows all the top brass at the Pentagon. The key point here... you never ever know.

Take some time away from yourself and offer to help someone else. Become a mentor to some young buck. You might find that young buck jumping higher than you ever thought possible... and taking you along with him!

TRADITIONAL NETWORKING:
"Waiting for someone else to help you become a success."

GUERRILLA NETWORKING:
"Helping someone else become a success before you."

TACTIC 33:
Invent Something Amazing

How many of you have watched late-night television and seen those commercials for a *free inventor's kit*? I am sure most of us have, or at least have some knowledge of them.

Why do these companies advertise on television? The answer is simple: some of the world's greatest inventions are inside the minds of regular television viewers who just happen to have 'an idea' to make the world a better place through a new product.

At Unstoppable Artists, all students and clients are encouraged and guided towards the creation of an invention. They are encouraged to believe that they have a wonderful idea (or 10!) inside their brains that is just waiting to come out with the proper encouragement. We encourage our students to create some new product or service that they can sell themselves, or license or sell to another company, thus becoming another stream of desperately needed income which can be used to produce their own artistic projects.

There is another reason, however, for recommending an invention. It is a perfect guerrilla networking strategy. Why? Because everyone wants to meet and hang out with 'an inventor'; with someone who holds a patent. It's *almost* as cool as being a published author! You become a rock star from another world. Someone who has contributed something magnificent to the world.

Here's the best part. Just holding the patent itself is a conversation starter. While you probably wouldn't want to spend the exorbitant fees on a patent unless the product idea itself had true marketability, it really doesn't even matter if the product is ever patented officially. Just being around someone who came up with an original idea and took the time to consider patenting it is an honor. Beyond that, though, holding a patent is truly an amazing accomplishment!

So get those mental gears turning, and open your eyes wide! Look at the world around you. Look where others are afraid to look. Look up. Down. Look left. Look right. Create a set of *inventor's eyes* and resolve to come up with at least 10 potential invention ideas this year. Then... go ahead. Request one of those free inventors kits. You might also call a patent attorney, or contact the patent office itself. Whatever you do, don't be scared, and just do it!

Consider this story: After my return from Iraq, I was really freaked out because I was reading *Backstage* (an acting trade newspaper) and noticed a bunch of copy-cat companies and books were popping up that were obviously inspired by Unstoppable Artists and my book *The Theatrical Juggernaut*. I became really concerned about sharing my ideas, and started to close off about sharing my thoughts about new film, tv, and music projects. Then, I called Jay to talk to him about it. He said, "Monroe, you should feel honored that people are stealing your ideas. If they aren't, that's when you should be worrying, because it means your ideas aren't any good." That made me feel really great, and now I look *forward* to people trying to do what I'm doing. (Note that I said *trying* — ha ha. No one helps artists succeed better than Monroe Mann!) Yet, as they say, imitation is the sincerest form of flattery, so I'll take that flattery from my competition every single day — it simply means my ideas are awesome.

TRADITIONAL NETWORKING:
"Always thinking, 'Hey, I thought of that!'"

GUERRILLA NETWORKING:
"Taking action on your thoughts before someone else beats you to it."

TACTIC 34:
Make Our Lives Easier

Thoreau once said, "If a man can write a better book, preach a better sermon, or make a better mouse trap than his neighbor, though he builds his house in the woods, the world will make a beaten path to his door." On the flip side to that argument, Edison countered, "It's not the best technology that gets accepted. It's the best promoted technology."

These two quotes resonate at the core of the 'talent' vs 'marketing' debate, and I was pleased to discover them side-by-side in my Masters of Entrepreneurship studies with Drs Jim & Joann Carland. It should be clear that Jay & I both believe that talent by itself is meaningless without the marketing and business prowess to back it up. As Robert Kiyosaki is fond of saying, "I'm not a best-*writing* author; I'm a best-*selling* author."

Nonetheless, there is truth in both of the quotations above, and if you can make our lives easier, better, more enjoyable, less stressful, happier, funnier, more productive, or more successful, people *will* want to meet you — as long as you market your product and/or services in the right manner. All types of people will want to get a piece of what you are offering. More people than you may know what to do with. More people than you may *want* to deal with.

Consider the 'trite and hackneyed' example of the Post-it® note. How utterly simple. And yet, did you come up with the idea? (Take note: if your answer is yes, you are either the inventor of the Post-it® note, and we congratulate you, or someone who came up with the idea, but didn't promote it well enough.) The point of the matter is that all you need to do is make our lives easier in some way, and people will like you more, and want to associate with you. It doesn't even need to be an 'invention', per se. It can be something as simple as helping someone carry the groceries, paying the toll for the person in the car behind you, or asking someone how their day was. Truly, it's often the little simple things that have the most impact.

Whatever it may be, just be sure it makes someone's life easier in some way. Strive every day to do something or think of something (and act on it) that will benefit someone else and make him smile with a sincere look of gratitude in his eyes.

TRADITIONAL NETWORKING:
"Wishing someone else would make life easier."

GUERRILLA NETWORKING:
"Making life easier yourself."

TACTIC 35:
Get Onto a Television Talkshow

Yup, here's another 'duh' suggestion, and yet, how many of you reading this were on a television show this past week? This past month? This past year?

To those who have, great! But are you scheduled to be on one tomorrow too? And next week? And is it nationally broadcast? Is it on TV5 in France, or RAI Uno in Italy? When was the last time you were on an international talk show in a foreign language?

Do you get the point? GET ONTO TV! GET ONTO TV! Heck, one appearance on television could make you the most desired person in the world! Or make your product or service the number one wish on everyone's Christmas list.

This is why you shouldn't roll your eyes when television is suggested. While the suggestion itself may be 'old news', the reality of the results should not be dismissed. Why are so many of you neglecting to use one of the most useful guerrilla networking principles?! If you want the very people you want to meet... to want to meet you, what better way then to get exposure to millions and millions of people through television? Your personality, speaking voice, good looks, and message all are disseminated at one time. What more can you ask for?

Bottom line: you should be doing everything within your power to become a guest on a major talk-show, and if that means starting small, via local cable access — wonderful! Do it! The sooner you begin practicing those interview skills, and amassing footage for your media demo reel, the more likely you'll soon be invited onto the nationals and/or *inter*nationals. And when that starts to happen... you'll have quite the large group of people calling you, emailing you, and banging down your door.

Note: you might notice that in this case, the talk show hosts and producers are the ones you first need to meet, and thus, need to convince to want to meet you. How do you do that? Simple: the answer is in your hands.

TRADITIONAL NETWORKING:
"Watching television."

GUERRILLA NETWORKING:
"Appearing on television."

TACTIC 36:
Get Referred

It really is sometimes hard to pitch the effectiveness of your own products and services in a believable manner. But if someone speaks about the benefits and accolades of your company on your behalf... it's a heck of a lot more believable.

Referrals are a beautiful thing. By having someone else talk you up, you become that much more the type of person other people want to meet.

Instead of trying to meet someone, a better strategy would be to — can you guess? — become the type of person that this person hopes to meet. One of the easiest and most effective ways of doing this is to have a mutual acquaintance open the door, and hold it for you, as you pass through and shake hands with the person you wanted to meet in the first place. Everything is easier when you have a smoothly functioning team on the case.

However, while referrals are one of those tools that are widely recognized as being a key to success, so very few people actually do what is necessary in order to secure them: ASK FOR THEM.

If you already have an established clientele of current and/or former clients/associates in the business... then it is your obligation to get over your fear of rejection and just call each of them up and ask for the names and phone numbers of three friends who might benefit from what you are offering. Or ask them to introduce you to so and so. If you are confident in who you are and what you have to offer, then you shouldn't have any issue asking for referrals... even from perfect strangers.

Too many people pursue referrals passively, and this doesn't work. You can't 'hope and pray' that people are going to talk you up to their friends. No one cares about you; they care about themselves. *You* need to be the one who ensures that referrals happen. *You* need to encourage others to introduce you to their friends and family. You have to ask for the referrals... and you need to do so without an ounce of hesitation, embarrassment, or self-consciousness.

Ask, and ye shall receive.

TRADITIONAL NETWORKING:
"Desperately trying to 'meet someone.'"

GUERRILLA NETWORKING:
"Enticing someone else to introduce you to that very same person."

TACTIC 37:
Get Out of the House

It is amazing how few people actually 'get out of the house', both literally and figuratively, and this has a profoundly negative impact on your networking success. Before you begin to misinterpret what this means by thinking we are encouraging you to 'go out and meet people', that is not the case. We are encouraging you to 'go out and show the world that you are someone she needs to meet."

From a literal standpoint, just think about how much time you are spending 'by yourself', i.e. at work behind your computer, at home on the couch, sitting quietly on the commuter train, etc. So many hours spent alone and self-absorbed, trying not to stand out, and not interacting with any other members of the human race. Sure, you are working to develop yourself and to become more successful, but if no one *knows* that you are doing these things, what's the point? You need to — literally — *GET OUT OF THE HOUSE!*

From a figurative standpoint, leave your "homepage"! Post blogs. Tell people what you are doing. Tell people what you are planning to do. Post news on your website. Create a monster-size email list and broadcast all the great things happening in your life. Do something radical. Get onto tv and radio. Give a speech. Write a book and get it published. Become a member of society! *GET OUT OF THE HOUSE!*

If you live life under a rock, you can be sure that few people are going to want to venture into your domain. However, if you come out into the sun, and into the public eye, you'll become more visible, and certainly more attractive. Few people want to deal with those who live in life's shadows, so live it up!

You need to 'boldly go where no man has gone before'. You need to take some chances. You need to risk ridicule.

You need to make it abundantly clear that you are an absolutely incredible member of the human race, and that associating with you will likely bring great rewards to those who do. The larger your efforts to 'get out of the house', the more quickly you'll find that the rest of the world wants to stop by and have dinner at that very house you just left.

TRADITIONAL NETWORKING:
"Waiting for success to knock on your door."

GUERRILLA NETWORKING:
"Opening the door to allow opportunity in."

TACTIC 38:
Tell People What You Are Going to Do

My oh my oh me oh my. There are way too many people in the world who subscribe to the belief that if you tell people what your plans are, they are going to steal the idea, ridicule you, or criticize you. Some believe that if they share their hopes, dreams, and ambitions with people... then they are bragging, and doing something rude, insensitive, and uncouth. Even more crazy, some actually believe that by proclaiming what they are going to do, they are somehow 'jinxing' any likelihood of success.

All of that is absurd, and frankly, simply a cover up of fear — and fear of accountability at that.

You see, when you share your plans with the world, or heck, even with your significant other or best friend, you have just done something that most people shun: created accountability. The more people with whom you share your plans... the more people there are who are counting on you to deliver. That's one reason why you should be telling as many people as possible about your plans: it helps force you to follow through.

Perhaps more importantly, there is absolutely *NO* way anyone can offer to help you unless they see that you need help, unless you ask for help, or unless they see such promise in what you are trying to do that they offer help unsolicited. In all cases, it's guerrilla networking at work: by telling people what you are going to do, you open up a world of possibility by potentially becoming the very person they want to meet. And that person is quite often the very person *you* want to meet as well. And you matched up with this person by simply proclaiming to the world your plans for the future.

True, there are those who are going to ridicule you, criticize you, and perhaps try to steal your idea. And some may consider you uncouth and a braggard. And sure, there is the chance that by sharing your plans, you actually turn some people away from you. Who cares about them? They are few and far between, and you're going to have to deal with these types of people for your entire life. Understand this: you are not sharing your plans to create criticism fodder for these people; you are sharing your plans in order to get across to the world that, "Hey, here I am, doing really cool things, and I'd really love your assistance and help, so if you've got any suggestions, ideas, or supportive solutions, let me know, ok?"

Go ahead and start spreading the word. To everyone and anyone you meet. You may be quite surprised with who ends up offering to help you.

TRADITIONAL NETWORKING:
"Keeping your ambition to yourself."

GUERRILLA NETWORKING:
"Having the guts to tell the world."

TACTIC 39:
Tell People What You Have Done

If you want people to meet you, just tell these people what you have done. What a brainstorm, huh?! What a novel concept. Well, consider this:

HAVE YOU ACTUALLY BEEN DOING IT ON A REGULAR BASIS?

In other words, have you been blabbing about your accomplishments like there's no tomorrow? Have you been telling everyone about all of the wonderful things you have accomplished? Yes, there is a fine line between 'sharing the vibe' — as I like to call it — and annoying and repulsive bragging, *and it's worth finding out what that line is.*

Your bottom line mission is getting people to want to meet you, right? Isn't it obvious that people are more likely to want to meet you and associate with you if you are someone of accomplishment? If you are someone who has actually *done* something? If you are someone who isn't ashamed of his accomplishments, and who isn't embarrassed to talk about them for fear of being branded arrogant and cocky and full of himself?

Here's some advice: GET OVER IT. Get over your fear of whether people like you or hate you. They are going to do that no matter what. It's better to be thought an arrogant success than a humble failure, don't you agree?

Yes, it is sometimes difficult to artfully share your accomplishments without appearing boorish. Alas, therein lies the reason why very few people are truly great networkers: they don't bother to take the time to learn the art. How do you *learn* the art? You learn the art by trying, failing, and finding the strength and courage to get up and try again.

TRADITIONAL NETWORKING:
"Bragging boastfully and crudely, making others feel inferior."

GUERRILLA NETWORKING:
"'Sharing the vibe' so others feel a part of your excitement and success, and feel they can be successful like you too."

TACTIC 40:
Tell People What You Are Currently Doing

Since we're on this kick of 'telling people', we'd be remiss if we didn't also remind you to tell people what you are *currently* doing. As in right now.

Here's a big hint: if you don't have a lot to discuss about what you're doing in the exact moment of here and now... then you really need to re-evaluate your guerrilla networking strategy.

You see, people want to hang out and work with and give money to people who are movers and shakers. Not 'has beens' who have long worn out their stories of past conquests, and not wannabes who constantly talk talk talk about what they're *going* to do in the future, but rarely actually do. People want to hang out and work with those who are *doers* — the movers and shakers of today who everyone wants to associate with.

So ask yourself: what am I *actually doing **right now*** that is cool, unexpected, exciting, impressive, new, different, and/or special? Make a list! Often we don't even realize how cool we really are, and we sell our accomplishments and our 'doings' short. Don't do that! Take some time to make a list of all of the cool things you are doing. Do it right now. In the margin. Go ahead, be a rebel and mark up the margins of the book with a list of all of the cool things you are doing. In fact, while you're at it, make a list of all the cool things you are doing, you have DONE, and yes, the things you are GOING TO DO.

Did you finish your list? It's longer than you thought, isn't it? And wow, aren't you cool after all?! Well, now the hard part begins: you need to make sure you have this list in your head at all times, because it is guaranteed that you are going to be asked the infamous question [So, what are you up to?] in the most unlikely of places and at the most unexpected of times. Whether you capitalize on these opportunities will be determined by how well you prepare for them.

TRADITIONAL NETWORKING:
"Keeping it to yourself so you don't jinx it."

GUERRILLA NETWORKING:
"'Telling everyone so others can jump on board."

TACTIC 41:
Thank Them... Again

Sure, we mentioned this earlier, but it bears repeating. Why? Because no one says thank you as much as they should, so we figured you needed a second reminder!

Truly, nothing costs so little, and can give you so much. Study after study has proven that most people quit their jobs due to feelings of under-appreciation. They say that their bosses didn't make them feel special, wanted, needed, and showed no gratitude for the work — however big — that they had done.

Well, that principle doesn't apply to just the work environment; it applies to your entire life in general! Everyone — read: *EVERYONE* — feels underappreciated. Girls. Boys. Men. Women. Astronauts. EVEN THE BOSS FEELS UNDERAPPRECIATED BY HIS EMPLOYEES! No matter how successful or how humble your standing in life, we know that you — yes you — have felt underappreciated at some point in the last few weeks. We're right on the money aren't we?

Well then, doesn't it stand to reason that by making it a habit to say thank you to people, repeatedly, over and over again, even for the simplest of things, and even at risk of constantly repeating yourself, that you are probably going to be building up a huge bank account of appreciation and respect from the people at the receiving end? And doesn't it stand to reason that this person would probably think of you for opportunities before others, simply because of your thoughtfulness?

Yes, Yes, YES!

It's a simple concept! But don't you get indignant and say, "Oh, I say thank you constantly." No matter: the truth of the matter is that you can say it one more time today than you usually do, and it won't cost you a dime, and it won't cost you more than a few seconds of your time. And yet... it just may make the difference.

TRADITIONAL NETWORKING:
"Being rude and insensitive."

GUERRILLA NETWORKING:
*"Realizing that you did **not** do it alone."*

TACTIC 42:
Do Something That No One Has Ever Done Before

Okay, this one is a tough one. It involves more risk and more guts than perhaps any of the other guerrilla networking techniques described in this book. For that reason, though, it is often one of the most effective: if you do something that no one has ever done before, people *will* want to meet you.

You see, the essence of guerrilla networking involves originality, and uniqueness. If you become someone original and unique (in a good way, of course), it helps you stand out in a crowd, and others will want to be by your side.

How do you become original and unique, then? Simple: *DO* something original and unique! Do something that no one has ever done before; that solves a problem of some sort; that makes peoples' lives easier in some way. Think of the light bulb and Thomas Edison; the iPod and Apple; the Post-It® Note by 3M. Services apply too, such as the Guerrilla Marketing franchise; the Unstoppable Artists business concept; and even the principle of guerrilla networking itself: this is truly a unique book in that very few, if any, networking books have ever discussed the subject in quite the way that we are doing here on these pages. We are doing *something that no one has ever done before...* and it is on that hope that we expect the book to do well. In fact, we are hoping that this idea of guerrilla networking is the type of idea that other people will want to read about, and that by association, we (Monroe and Jay) are going to become the type of people others want to meet — or more so, as the case may truthfully be.

There is a book that we all have heard of called *The Guinness Book of World Records*. How do people get into that book? By doing something that no one has ever done before. There's an interesting connection here. Those people in that book often get a lot of media attention just for even *attempting* to break the world record (as you'll discover in Part III of this book.)

So whaddya know: guerrilla networking works.

TRADITIONAL NETWORKING:
"Coloring within the lines on the piece of paper."

GUERRILLA NETWORKING:
"'Turning the paper into an airplane."

TACTIC 43:
Do Something Better

Want people to want to meet you? There's an old saying that 'you can't improve on perfection'. Well, here's the reality: nothing is ever perfect, so if you can be the one to 'perfect perfection', then you'll be in quite the powerful position.

Sure, just because you build the better mousetrap, doesn't mean people are going to clammer to your door, but it certainly does make it more likely.

Remember the definition of guerrilla networking: becoming the type of person other people want to meet. Other people. Becoming the type of person other people want to meet.

Okay, so look at what's going on in your industry, your school, your business, you place of work, your household. Can you improve on the way something is being done. Or, do you have the solution to something that is just *not working right*?

This principle here is the key to success in service marketing: you identify a problem that a prospect is having, and clearly explain that you can show them a solution, and a better way to do what they are doing. Voila! If you close the sale properly, they will — ta da! — want to meet you (and give you their money)!

The key is in the communication and the delivery: people need to actually see, believe, and trust that what you are offering is better that what is currently being offered, or what is currently being done. If you offer better service, better quality, better customer service, better price — all other things being equal — you are *going* to be able to attract people and customers to you and to your place of business who might ordinarily not consider you.

Just keep thinking to yourself as you make your way through your day: can I do that better? How can I do this better? In what way can I do this better?

TRADITIONAL NETWORKING:
"Stopping at 'good enough.'"

GUERRILLA NETWORKING:
"'Always striving to be better."

TACTIC 44:
Hitch Your Wagon to a Star

Who is Monroe Mann? Well, if you didn't know me — Monroe — before picking up this book, you certainly know me today as the co-author of this fine publication. And this newfound interest in meeting me is probably a result of my co-authoring this book with Jay, right?

BINGO.

Hitch your wagon to a star.

If you want to succeed in the world of guerrilla networking, you first need to acknowledge that you are probably not as well known as you would like to be (and need to be!) That being established, the quickest way to increase the number of people who want to meet you is... to partner up with a bigger name.

I could certainly have written and published a networking book on my own. The question is... how many people would have bought it? Sure, I would have sold a couple thousand copies to my own circle of fans and readers, but I probably wouldn't have reached even an 1/8th of how many people are reading this book now. This book, more than likely, is in you hands not because of me, but rather because there is another — far more prominent — name preceding mine on the front cover of this book: none other than that of the master himself, Jay Conrad Levinson.

On that note, you might be intrigued to know that originally, the order of the names on the front cover was to be Monroe Mann followed by Jay Conrad Levinson. Jay had no issue with that, but he did make a poignant comment: "Monroe, I'm fine with whichever order you prefer, because I want to help you, but think about this: who is the bigger 'movie star' of books right now?" He was right. The answer, of course, is Jay Conrad Levinson.

He went on to make the correct observation that more people will trust — and thus purchase — the book if his name were first. As a result, more people would then know my name, Monroe Mann. And then, well, that's guerrilla networking in action folks. Here you are, reading this book: *Guerrilla Networking* by Jay Conrad Levinson & Monroe Mann!

Now, your turn. Think about your industry and make a list of the 'movie stars' of your industry. Who would you be proud to have your name next to? What company might give your own credibility a boost were they to associate with you?

Again, the key is to get over your ego, first and foremost. Yes, we know that you can do it 'on your own', but how *well* can you do it on your own? Now that is the true question. You might be able to find a 20% solution on your own, but by partnering up with a bigger name, you are far more likely to find the 80% solution that is going to bring in big bucks, big recognition, and big satisfaction.

Don't try to do it solo. Try to get as many people involved with your projects as possible. The more successful and recognizable names you can attach to you and/or your projects, the more likely other successful and recognizable names will want to jump on board as well.

Now, is it easy to hitch your wagon to a star? In many ways, yes it is. You just have to keep you eyes open, don't let your ego blind you, and remember to ASK! On the other hand, it is not necessarily an easy thing to do. It may take persistence, time, and a lot of hard work... but in the end, it'll be a heck of a lot easier than trying to 'establish yourself' on your own. That could take a lifetime, and unfortunately, that's all we have! By hitching your wagon to a star, you'll end up establishing yourself long before that lifetime of yours is over.

TRADITIONAL NETWORKING:
"Going it alone."

GUERRILLA NETWORKING:
"'Putting your ego to the side."

TACTIC 45:
Give Them What They Want

I t's a not-so-strange phenomenon that when you give people what they want... they tend to want to be associated with you.

Guerrilla networking — at its core — is basically just presenting yourself and your services in such a way that everyone else thinks they need whatever it is you are offering. A surefire way to ensure this is to first figure out *what they specifically want* in the first place, and then, deliver!

Think about the logic of this. Instead of trying to PUSH your product or service onto the uninterested consumer, you often will have more success if you use a PULL marketing strategy that actually pulls them into the store. That is what you are doing with guerrilla networking! Instead of trying to push yourself and your services onto others, i.e. *meeting people*, you are working to pull those very same people towards you, i.e. *by becoming the type of person that other people want to meet!*

Think of the people you most want to meet. Are they customers? Are they prospects? Are they politicians? Are they agents or managers? Are they record labels, film companies, marketing firms, publicists, accountants, what? Who is it that you are most interested in meeting?

Once you have that established, the next step is to simply figure out what they want. Sure, it's a lot easier said than done, but that is the key. Take the time to really figure out what it is these people most want. Hint: usually it's money; but not always.

Once you make that list, the next step is to rack your brain to determine how you can fulfill that need. We assure you: if you can fulfill that need, and make it clear that you are the best person to fulfill that need, then making the 'sale' will be one of the easiest things you've ever done.

TRADITIONAL NETWORKING:
"Giving them what you think they need."

GUERRILLA NETWORKING:
"Giving them what they actually want."

TACTIC 46:
Solve a Problem

Oh how simple guerrilla networking is! Yes, this is number 46. Solve a problem. That's our advice — and it's good advice too!

You see, every major invention in this world; every major break-through; every multi-million dollar success story — they all have a common thread; and that common thread is the solution to a prob-lem. If you can solve problems; you can make millions. Truly, if you are solving problems and making millions... then getting people to want to meet you is a very simple straight-forward task indeed.

So think about it. Open your eyes. What problems are you and others facing on a daily, weekly, or monthly basis? Can you come up with a novel and original solution to those problems? Sure you can! Just grab a pad and paper, keep these tools with you constantly, and jot down ideas as they come to you throughout the day. Some of the ideas may seem foolish to you, but write them down anyway. The key is to get your 'problem solving skills' trained up. Before you know it, you'll start to see opportunity for problem solving everywhere.

This principle applies in your regular business, and in your personal life too. Offer to (and prove that you can) solve someone else's problem, and that person will want to meet you. Guaranteed. No ifs, ands, or buts. Want more business? Make it clear that you can solve a tangible problem someone has. Want more friends? Try to reach out to people and offer a caring ear; become that 'someone to talk to' that we all seek to have.

But solving one single problem often isn't the be all and end all. To truly make an impact, you should be striving to solve *many* problems. The more problems you solve, the more people are going to want to meet you. It's simple probability, and you should exploit that fact for everything it is worth.

TRADITIONAL NETWORKING:
"Coming up with the problems."

GUERRILLA NETWORKING:
"'Solving them."

TACTIC 47:
Be Useful

Too many people forget that one of the keys to success is usefulness. In many ways, usefulness is related to uniqueness, originality, education, knowledge, connections, etc. Whatever it is that defines 'usefulness', the underlying theme is that you are indispensable.

If you are indispensable, it means that a business, enterprise, or individual, is not capable of operating at peak efficiency (if at all) without your help, assistance, and guidance. One of the keys to avoiding being fired from a job, or to avoid going out of business if you are an entrepreneur, is to become indispensable — and in order to be indispensable, you first need to be useful.

In other words, you cannot be extra baggage. You cannot be extra baggage in a business, or in someone's life. In either case, you will eventually be discarded, sold, or traded. *You do not want this to happen!* In fact, your mission as a guerrilla networker is to become so useful and so indispensable that *other* companies and people start vying for your attention; that you are now actually being *pulled* in five different directions because so many people want you all to themselves! Ahh, what a beautiful thought, yes?

And it can happen! It can become true! All you need to do is figure out how to become more useful and indispensable in the minds of others. Right now, if you are not meeting the people you want to meet, and you are not attracting the right kind of crowd, there is only one diagnosis: they don't consider what you offer to be indispensable, and they don't consider you yourself to be all that useful in their lives.

Putting it in the above blunt terms might seem harsh, but it's the truth and fact of the matter. If you are not succeeding as you think you should be, and are not hanging out and working with the types of people you feel you should be associating with, the problem is you. While you may be a really wonderful person to meet, the problem lies in the fact that *the other people for some reason don't think so.* And if such is the case, then the problem very well may be... your marketing *and* your networking. Hint: Read *Guerrilla Marketing, 4th edition!* And then re-read this book again from the beginning.

Remember: it doesn't matter if *you* think you are useful; what matters if *other people* think you are useful. Convincing them of that fact is the challenge, and the adventure!

TRADITIONAL NETWORKING:
"Wasting time, energy, and resources."

GUERRILLA NETWORKING:
"'Not doing that."

TACTIC 48:
Be The Answer to Their Prayers

Everyone needs help, and everyone is struggling in some way, shape, or form. For some, it is a question of finances. For others, a question of not enough publicity. For still others, loneliness, or lack of courage, or lack of focus and direction, or maybe, the need for support. Maybe they are looking for the answer to a really tough question.

Whatever it may be, there is *no one* on this planet who is completely happy, secure, and has every single thing that he needs or is hoping for. We are human, and we all have our struggles. Therefore, if you can be the answer to those prayers and hopes... then you're practicing guerrilla networking.

In this situation, the key is to listen. You can't be the answer to someone's prayers if you don't know what those prayers are! So listen up. Listen for what they are crying out for. What *are* their prayers? What is it that they are hoping, praying, reaching, and crying out for?

It's true! People are crying out for help every day. Have you not noticed? All you have to do is be aware of this fact, and then strive to make a difference in the lives of these people.

Just think for a moment about the people in your life, and that includes those very people you hope to meet. What would be the answer to their prayers? For Apple computers, it would be a mass migration to the iMac. For Microsoft, it would be the exact opposite. For an actor, it would be the role of a lifetime, or even just a leg up. And for an entrepreneur, it would be a loan for $200,000... that doesn't need to be paid back!

Just think! These prayers from the people of the world are ricocheting in and around your head right now. Just reach out, grab a few, and see what they say. Then match up those prayers with the people who originated them... and *deliver!*

Nothing in the world will bring a bigger smile to someone's face than being the answer to a prayer. Be a guerrilla, and be that answer to someone's prayer. You'll be pleasantly surprised with the results.

TRADITIONAL NETWORKING:
"Praying for a solution."

GUERRILLA NETWORKING:
"Becoming the answer to someone else's prayer."

TACTIC 49:
Name Drop!

Yes, yes, there is a negative stigma associated with 'name dropping', but here's the truth of the matter: if done properly, no one considers it name dropping. Name dropping is simply the sleazy term given to what I call 'strategic name placement'. Or rather, 'name dropping' is what happens when you use 'strategic name placement' in the wrong way, shape, manner, or place.

We decided to mention this tactic because far too many people are under the impression that 'name dropping' is bad form. Not so! Done correctly, strategic name placement can open up doors, seal the deal, and well... entice the very people you want to meet, to want to meet you!

So, how to do it properly? You need to weave the person's name into the conversation or pitch in such a way that it builds credibility and adds to what you are saying; it has to be so inextricably linked to what you are talking about that it doesn't appear to be coming out of left field. If the person you are 'pitching' to feels even remotely that you are mentioning the name simply as a way to network your way into their heart... you lose. They will call your bluff, and you won't make much headway.

However, if in the course of your pitch and/or conversation, you subtly (but directly, and with cool crisp confidence) mention the name of someone whose reputation is more well known and respected than yours — and make it clear that you are genuinely and closely associated with this person — you'll do nothing but help your cause. For example, when I mention that I am a published author to people, the next question is inevitably, "Oh, what have you written?" You see, their question just opened the door for strategic name placement, and my response lately has been, "A bunch of attitude and business books; my latest is a book I am co-writing with Jay Conrad Levinson; you know him — the guy who wrote *Guerrilla Marketing*."

Their response?

"Oh yeah! I know that book! Awesome! Wow! That's pretty impressive!"

And bingo... I just scored some major cool points thanks to the principle of guerrilla networking: becoming the type of person that *other* people want to meet. And all thanks to what people derisively call 'name dropping'.

Remember, done properly, you should consider it 'strategic name placement'.

TRADITIONAL NETWORKING:
"Name Dropping."

GUERRILLA NETWORKING:
"'Strategic Name Placement."

TACTIC 50:
Be a Guerrilla

After all is said and done, guerrilla networking — *becoming the type of person other people want to meet* — comes down to one simple action that you need to do on a daily basis:

Determine what other people are looking for, and give them what they want.

When you think about it, that is the *essence* of success in the world of entrepreneurship, and in fact, in life. If you can satisfy what other people want and give them what they are looking for... then you win. In business. In relationships. In life. It's all the same: if you become the type of person that they are looking for... and make it as easy as possible for these people to find you... you win. Voila!

When we encourage you to 'be a guerrilla', we mean that you need to think outside of the box. Whatever everyone else is doing, do the opposite. Be a rebel. Live dangerously. Grab life by the horns and don't take no for an answer.

Therefore, it doesn't matter which strategies you decide to use; the most important thing to realize is simply that each strategy indicates the very same way of thinking you need to embrace in order to get noticed, and become the type of person/establishment that others want to meet, hire, and heck — even fall in love with.

You see, this list of 50 guerrilla networking strategies is far from complete. There are certainly hundreds more to be developed, mined, and used (and you'll read about some of them in the next part of this book.) What you just read is just a list *to get you started*. They are a ton more guerrilla networking strategies you can come up with if you simply embrace and brainstorm off the central idea of guerrilla networking: becoming the type of person other people want to meet.

In other words, understanding guerrilla networking will do nothing for you. Rather, it's your passion and patience for the implementation of guerrilla networking that will ultimately determine if you make it to the finish line; for before others will make efforts to come to you, you need to first — like it or not — make effort to *impress them*. And that takes hard work.

While most people (and networking texts) continue to tell you that networking is about getting in front of the right people, getting people to take your calls, and getting 'out there', we disagree. Being a guerrilla means enticing the right people to fight to get in front of *you*; about enticing the people you want to meet to call *you*; and about getting all those people 'out there', clamoring and fighting to get 'in here' — right into your office, your life, and your inner circle.

TRADITIONAL NETWORKING:
"Meeting people."

GUERRILLA NETWORKING:
"Becoming the type of person other people want to meet."

PART 3

Guerrilla Networking in Action

INTRODUCTION:
Guerrilla Networking in Action

What follows is an inspiring and instructive collection of guerrilla networking stories. Some are from very prominent people; others from up and comers — all have benefited from the power of guerrilla networking. We chose to incorporate a variety of different people from many different walks of life in this collection because guerrilla networking is a concept everyone can use to get ahead. 'Becoming the type of person others want to meet' is not a lofty idea that only works for those who have already accomplished great things, but rather, a simple concept that everyone can benefit from, and yes, that includes YOU!

Jay Conrad Levinson	*Author & Business Coach*
Ned Vizzini	*Author & Musician*
Andrew Young	*Counterintelligence Officer, US Army*
Carol Blaha	*Independent Sales Rep & Sales Trainer*
Arthur Brown	*Comedian, Actor, & Author*
James Dillehay	*Author & Business Coach*
Barry Morgenstein	*Photographer*

Kathy Hagenbuch	*Business Coach*
Debbie Bordelon	*Food Services Manager*
Graham Guerra	*Fine Artist & Professor*
Ashley Ann Serafin	*Customer Service Manager & Actor*
Knox Vanderpool	*Business Owner*
Paul Rieckhoff	*Not-For-Profit Business Owner*
Bones Rodriguez	*Actor, Author, and Entrepreneur*
Dennis Hurley	*Actor & Screenwriter*
Phil Malandrino	*Business Owner, Actor, & Producer*
Douglas C. Williams	*Actor, Singer, & Entrepreneur*
Roberta Muse	*Politician & French Teacher*
Kip Gienau	*Ad Agency Owner & Author*
Marcia Harp	*Actress & Singer*
Scott duPont	*Actor & Producer*
Kolie Crutcher	*Electrical Engineer, Actor, & Author*
Ed Smith	*TV Show Host & Author*
Scott Norman	*Actor & Producer*
Peter Bielagus	*Financial Advisor, Speaker, & Author*
Monroe Mann	*Author, Musician, Actor, & Business Coach*

NOTE: *After you finish reading the great stories that follow, we look forward to helping you put together your **own** guerrilla networking strategy in Section IV... Keep reading! There's lots more ahead...*

JAY CONRAD LEVINSON

My networking in Chicago during the sixties helped get me to where I am, but none of it happened due to planning; I was guerrilla networking without even realizing it.

Some of it happened because of my love for San Francisco, where I had just left. Some happened due to skiing because I met a group of eight who shared my passion for the slopes. Some took place because of my penchant for playing softball, motivating me to join a team, play against other teams, and meet a lot of fascinating people.

The social outgrowths of these non-business networking opportunities meant my wife and I were invited to more parties where we met more people. Eventually I found myself in a conversation with two guys who worked at my dream advertising agency: Leo Burnett. They were equally intrigued that I was a writer and invited me to come in and interview and to mention their names.

Three years later, I was a member of the board and creative director of Leo Burnett in London.

The path from Comiskey Park to Hyde Park was neither a direct one, nor a plannable one, and I would not have traded one step. Not one. But it is undeniable that I am where I am because of the choices I made; and those choices made me someone that others wanted to meet.

AUTHOR BIOGRAPHY: Jay Conrad Levinson is the author of over 43 books, with over 15 million copies sold in over 43 languages. He is known the world over as the 'father of guerrilla marketing'. His contact information can be found at the beginning of this book.

NED VIZZINI

When I began my writing career, I decided to treat it like an indie band. I knew that no one knew about me and that it would be an uphill fight to get people to learn about my books and take me seriously.

So I made flyers. I gave them out wherever I could. I went to readings or to shows where people who might like my book were gathered. When I went to the shows, I always said — "Buy my book. It's like the Green Day of books." Or something similar. It really worked for every band.

I also made a database of people who I knew in publishing. It started out as a very small database! It consisted mostly of people who my parents knew: very few. But then it started to expand. And every time I met someone (like Monroe!), I put that person in the database and have done my best to stay in touch with them over the years with notes, emails, and invitations to parties.

The end result: My work has been honored by the American Library Association, BookSense, and the New York Public Library, has been translated into five languages (forthcoming in Chinese), and my latest book, *It's Kind of a Funny Story*, has been called "insightful and utterly authentic" by the *NY Times Book Review*.

So never underestimate the importance of a flyer, and the willingness of people to help you as long as you are open and honest about what you want to achieve. People will support someone who they see as being in a possible position in the future to help them back. Even if you're the guy just starting out who no one knows about, if you can convince others that you're going places, you'll be amazed at the credibility that will give you going forward.

AUTHOR BIOGRAPHY: Ned Vizzini is the author of *It's Kind of a Funny Story, Be More Chill, and Teen Angst? Naaah...*, the last of which he wrote and published while he was 19 years old. He lives in Brooklyn, NY, and once played bass in Monroe's band. He can be reached via: nvizzini@gmail.com or www.nedvizzini.com.

ANDREW YOUNG

After leaving the Army in 1995, I began working at a major air express company on 39th Street in Manhattan. I accepted the position to gain industry and operations experience while I searched for something in the Albany, NY area, where my wife and I had our primary residence. While working in the City Monday to Thursday, I stayed with my parents in Ossining, NY. Needless to say, it was tough on us "newlyweds," but we knew it would not last forever.

While I worked in the City, I searched for companies I wanted to work for in Albany. Unfortunately, it was a small market with primarily retail and government jobs available. Through word of mouth, though, I soon heard of a division of PepsiCo, Inc which had a major operation in the Guilderland Center area. This was the town we lived in. The plant, which employed approx 200 employees, was the servicing distribution center for all the Pepsi owned restaurants in the Northeast. The company served 861 Taco Bell, KFC, and Pizza Hut restaurants from New York City to Maine. This was a tremendous operation with endless opportunity. I was determined to see if I could get hired by Pepsi.

I was confident my experience in NYC combined with my union and delivery experience would be a "win, win" situation for both of us. I contacted the PepsiCo Distribution Manager. After four phone calls, he agreed to review my resume. Of course I got the typical answer: "Although your resume is impressive, I regret we have no present openings in the Operations or Transportation Departments. I will forward your resume to our corporate HR dept in Texas in case the corporation has any future openings."

Brick Wall. Next step, I thanked the Distribution Manager and asked him if he'd be willing to meet with me for lunch or breakfast. I wanted to at least express my desire to work for PepsiCo in person. Unfortunately, after numerous unsuccessful phone calls, I realized that I was striking out badly and simply continued to work at my air express job, trying to hatch another plan in the meantime.

Well, I usually had to be to work in Manhattan at 2 PM daily. So, on a Monday morning I drove to Pepsi at 0800. I waited for the Distribution Manager to arrive at work and waited to introduce myself. At first he appeared shocked and surprised to see me, but then he invited me in. He said he had no time for breakfast, but did have a few minutes to chat.

I shared my background in the US Army as an officer and my logistical experiences in Operation Desert Storm. He was impressed with what I had accomplished so far and with how I was traveling back and forth to Manhattan even though I was recently married and living in the Albany area. But he still said he had no present openings.

With nothing else to lose, I went for it! I offered to work at the company for "free" (no salary) as long he would fairly evaluate my skills and management potential. At the end of the negotiated time frame, if he was not satisfied, I would thank him for the opportunity and he would never hear from me again. He said my proposal (if accepted) would be an extremely unorthodox working relationship. He said he would have to think about it and discuss it with his Regional Manager. I naturally took that as the corporate blow off, thanked him for his time, and drove to New York City once again for my shift.

I did not hear from PepsiCo for 30 days, and by this time, I had already 'moved on' in my mind. But then one day my wife received a phone call. It was the Distribution Manager; He wished to speak with me ASAP!

Amy called me at my parents on a Wednesday night. I immediately called the Distribution Manager. But, unfortunately, it wasn't the message I wanted to hear. The Manager said it was against company policy to hire someone and have them work without compensation for any length of time. Therefore, the "tryout" would not be an option. That was incredibly disappointing.

Instead, though, he offered me an Operations Manager job in the Transportation Department, at $10K over my present salary, *and* a $4K signing bonus! He said that due to my unyielding desire to take no for an answer, my initiative, and my dedication shown by my working in New York City, I was just the type of young manager he wanted servicing his customers.

My Mom, Dad, and I shared a huge bottle of champagne that night. I did it! I scored a major operations gig at a Fortune 500 company, five miles from my apartment. The hard work and sacrifice paid off.

I guess the lesson here is: "When you want something, go for it! Market yourself, do not get discouraged, and keep pushing. Your desire will break down bureaucratic barriers and prove to people you have the desire to succeed... resulting in you becoming the type of person they want to hire and work with."

I stayed with the company for 2 years, was promoted twice, and we made Pepsi a considerable amount of money. When PepsiCo decided to sell off its food service division to a local vendor, it was time for me to leave. It was a great experience and I learned a lot about personnel management, marketing, and customer service. Time well spent.

I always laugh when I eat at Pizza Hut, KFC, or Taco Bell, and hear the kids complain about working there for $7 per hour. I was willing to do it for *free!*

AUTHOR BIOGRAPHY: Major Andrew Young is a 13-year counterintelligence officer, and a veteran of Operation Iraqi Freedom (serving with Monroe Mann) and also Desert Storm. He holds a masters degree from SUNY, Albany, and a BA from SUNY Binghamton, and is currently working on an autobiography. He lives in northern Virginia with his wife and three kids. He can be contacted by email via andrew.young1@us.army.mil or by phone via 518-221-1429.

CAROL BLAHA

My favorite tool from the guerrilla networking toolbox is establishing myself as a resource to my clients. To that end, I make it very clear that my position is to make my clients money. When you make clients money, they will swarm to you.

What do I do? I own a manufacturer's representative agency selling floor coverings. One of my products is residential and commercial carpet. For those not in the industry, carpet is often considered to be a commodity because it is often sold and compared by face weight. In addition, there is huge competition by some very well known and well marketed companies such as Shaw, owned by Warren Buffet. Finally, like in any other commodity sale, there are few differentiators with actual measurable differences.

I knew I couldn't compete on price or variety; my competitors paid rebates and offered co-op dollars that I couldn't touch. I couldn't convince retailers to stock my product either. They consistently shut me out; convinced that an unknown with a higher price was not saleable, and certainly not worth any time or floor space.

However, I knew that my product had warranties that were measurable benefits to the end users. Moreover, these benefits truly differentiated my products from my competitors. "If only I could reach the end users," I thought to myself. And that's when the tide began to turn.

At the time, I was having a particular problem in a smaller Colorado town. On my next trip, instead of retailers, I met with the major end users, demonstrating the benefits and performance of the product. After creating interest, I ended each call with the question, "What retailer do you work with?" I then went to those retailers, confidently saying, "I have met with your major consumer in the area, and they want this product — should I refer them to you as carrying the line?"

You bet the answer was yes! In fact, because the major users bid to more than one supplier — I ended up having multiple retailers asking me to bring my product into their store. Soon, I actually had to limit distribution, cutting off the number of retailers I would sell to, because some of the stores wanted exclusivity.

The moral of the story is this: you can become the type of person retailers want to work with by becoming the type of person end users want to buy from.

AUTHOR BIOGRAPHY: Carol Blaha is the owner of an independent manufacturer's rep agency specializing in environmentally conscious flooring solutions. Her manufacturers include Kraus Carpet Mills, Parterre, Lonseal, Permagrain, Imagine Tile, and Capri Cork. She is also a sales trainer, mentor, and business consultant and developer of the automatic salesperson program — the latte factor of sales.

Carol@automaticsalesperson.com
www.carolblaha.com

www.automaticsalesperson.com

303-684-9211 303-485-6326 FAX

1630 Amherst Dr, Longmont, CO 80503

ARTHUR BROWN

In 1991 I came up with the idea of writing the first guide to vegetarian restaurants in New York City. I entitled it, "Vegetarian Dining in NYC — and Not Just the Places the Yuppies Like". The book was unique. It was a contribution, and it was news.

Why the subtitle? First, I am a comedian. Why say something directly when I can joke about it? Second, I needed a hook.

From the outset, the whole project seemed natural: I'm a vegetarian and my family and I ate out a lot. Since no one told me I couldn't write this book, I went ahead and wrote it, edited it, published it (found and contracted with a printer), and began to bring copies around to all the "natural" bookstores.

The book was actually doing pretty well given my grass roots efforts, but I realized I needed to think bigger. I needed more people to know about this book.

So, I researched how to write press releases. On my first go-round, I sent out about a dozen press releases to about a dozen media outlets, including *The NY Times* (specifically Florence Fabricant who wrote a "What's New" column every Wednesday), and a food critic from *NY Newsday* who I had bumped into when we were both researching restaurants in little India. I also sent a press release to Arthur Schwartz at the *Daily News* — who had a radio show on WOR.

To my pleasure and astonishment, it worked. I got write ups all over town. The one-paragraph mention in The *NY Times* brought me hundreds of orders from all over the country. A full page story with photo followed in *Newsday*, and we were off to the races.

Each publicity package I sent out mentioned and included the previous articles, stories, photos, etc., and soon, I was gaining momentum, and using that momentum. Legitimacy built on legitimacy.

Soon, other media outlets including *WOR Radio, NY One Television*, and *Good Day NY* contacted me. Suddenly, I was the expert! Other authors (carnivorous and otherwise) wanted to meet me. I had done something. I was no longer going after them. They were coming after me. Hooah!

In closing, what can you, dear reader, learn from my veggie-tale? Just this: Become the Big cheese. Who cares if they think you're nuts? Don't chicken out, because as soon as they see you as the sauce, you'll be cookin'! And then they'll all want to meat you. So don't be sheepish — or you'll wind up with a lifetime of lamb-ents — and that, my fine friend, will cost you a mint.

AUTHOR BIOGRAPHY: Comedian, Author, Lyricist and Singer, Art Brown is a native New Yorker as well as a Father, Husband and Entrepreneur. He's been performing since the age of 12 and for three years, was a lyricist with the BMI/Lehman Engel Musical Theatre workshop. Art is the author of *Vegetarian Dining in NYC, Good and Cheap Dining in NY*, and the soon to be released, *Everything I Need to Know, I Learned from Cartoons*. He's also the co-star of the blockbuster film, *Origami Deathmatch*. In addition, Art is a client/student of Unstoppable Artists. To learn more about this charming and wonderful fellow, kindly visit: www.ArthurSBrown.com, or to have him build you a website, visit ArtBrownArt.biz. To say howdy and tell him how much you've always admired his work, the email is: me@arthursbrown.com

JAMES DILLEHAY

I grew and continue to build my networks using the endlessly effective tactic of guerrilla generosity, which is an obvious outreach of guerrilla networking.

In the process of authoring several books on marketing for artists and craftspeople, I've accumulated a substantial number of resources helpful to creative people. By listing myself online as an expert willing to help others, I receive requests for answers to questions every week. It only takes a few minutes of my time, but saves readers hours of searching.

The result of giving away this free and helpful advice has been that people sign up for my newsletter (also free,) tell their friends, and recommend me online in various places. A recent search for my name ("James Dillehay" in quotations) returns close to 10,000 mentions of my books and articles.

All of this contributes to sales of books, invitations for paid speaking engagements, article requests from magazines, a television appearance, and the list goes on. It works so well that I continually strive to apply generosity as a guerrilla networking tactic in everything I do, as often as I can, without seeking anything in return. The result: lots of people end up wanting to meet me.

AUTHOR BIOGRAPHY: James Dillehay is the author of seven books, and co-author of *Guerrilla Multilevel Marketing* with Jay Conrad Levinson. James' books have been recommended in *The Chicago Tribune, Family Circle, Entrepreneur Radio, Working Mothers,* and more. He is a former magazine editor and publisher and a Certified Guerrilla Marketing Coach.

james@gmmlm.com

www.jamesdillehay.com

www.gmmlm.com

www.craftmarketer.com

BARRY MORGENSTEIN

My name is Barry Morgenstein, and I am a headshot photographer for actors, models, and celebrities in New York City. My girlfriend and I were watching a 20/20 special with Diane Sawyer one night. The special centered on kids who live in Camden, NJ, one of the most dangerous cities in the US.

These kids wanted to make a better life for themselves. All the stories touched us, but one story caught my eyes. It spoke of Billy Joe Marrero, a young man who wanted to help his family get out of this dangerous neighborhood. He thought he might be able to make extra money by pursuing acting. He went to Philadelphia where they were casting for the new *Rocky* movie. The director refused to see him, since he did not have headshots.

I turned to my girlfriend and said, "I'm going to shoot his headshots for him." It seemed that — in a small way — this would be the best way for me to help.

So, I contacted the producers of 20/20 and offered my services for free. They in turn contacted Billy Joe Marrero. When he found out, he was overjoyed, and we went forward with plans for the shoot. I was not looking for publicity, but only wanted to help, and I was very excited about the shoot. It turned out, though, that *Fox News* heard of the story through the grapevine and decided to cover the photo shoot.

On the big day, *Fox* indeed showed up with cameras of their own, and we all had a great time together. The story aired on Fox and everyone at *ABC* was thrilled. It really felt good to do something for someone who needed help. And as a result, I ended up hearing from so many people that I didn't even know.

Moreover, the link to the story is on my website, so those who didn't see that actual broadcast are able to see the story when they visit my website. Many have seen the story, and in turn have then wanted to work with me, and meet me. In addition, I was happy to see that Billy Joe himself received an offer from a talent agency, and from a talent agency that now also helps me get more work.

As my makeup artist Maureen Walsh (who also volunteered) said to me, "Sometimes just doing good deeds with unselfish motives will bring people to you..."

AUTHOR BIOGRAPHY: Barry Morgenstein is one of the premier headshot photographers in New York. His photographs have appeared in *Rolling Stone*, *New York Magazine*, *The New York Times*, *People*, *Entertainment Weekly*, *Creem*, *Billboard*, *Parade*, and *Soap Opera Digest*. Some of the celebrities he has photographed include Arnold Schwarzenegger, Michael Jackson, Olympia Dukakis, Sarah Ferguson (the Duchess of York), Howard Stern, and yes, Monroe Mann. More information at www.BarryMorgenstein.com, and he can be reached at bmfoto6858@aol.com.

KATHY HAGENBUCH

As a very fast-paced, bottom-line, results-oriented person, getting what I wanted was never a problem. However, doing so in a way that actually encouraged others to want to help *me*, send business to me, etc. was a very foreign concept. Over the years, though, I have thankfully learned and implemented numerous skills and strategies that have made me more 'attractive' — to both clients and friends in general.

One of those strategies was to slow down and take a genuine interest in those I encountered. Since my natural style was fast-paced and bottom-line-results oriented, I tried to slow down and focus on asking questions and truly listening to the conversation. Instead of my normal 'multi-tasking' focus of thinking ahead to my next move, I took a greater interest in those I was speaking to.

Utilizing this essential communication skill allowed others to feel heard and respected. This new interaction allowed me to learn what was important to others (which is in many cases more important than what's important to me.) This allowed me to develop deep and meaningful relationships with those I associated, which translated to more sales.

As I continued to look for ways to attract people to me, I was reminded of a quote I had heard: 'If you can do it all yourself, your dream is not big enough'.

It then occurred to me that the smartest people I know all acknowledge that they do not know everything and can't do everything themselves, and seek to fill in those knowledge and ability gaps with people who excel in these areas. And as Robert Kiyosaki said, "The richest people in the world build networks. Everyone else is trained to look for work."

My mind once again stimulated, I finally started using the Six Figure Success Team Builder System I had developed and taught my small business clients to use. I eagerly started filling the eight categories of my Success Team with extraordinary people whose brilliance and talents complimented my own. With my imagination activated, I creatively combined the knowledge of how people were naturally wired and the simple automated systems from my 'Create Six Figures by Putting Your Business on Autopilot' program to build a strong and loyal team that allowed me to stand out from the crowd with professional lead generation and informative prospecting follow up, exceptional customer service and outstanding team support.

The magical result was that those in my network became motivated and inspired to send me referrals and business because they found that being part of my success directly resulted in achieving their own goals and dreams as well.

Finally, while it's important to be serious about your work — and that in itself has made me someone that others want to meet — it is just as important to have fun! It's just as important to be my normal bold, daring, outrageous self — and have fun! That's what others want to be part of. Fun.

As Dale Carnegie once said, "People rarely succeed unless they have fun in what they are doing." While our future and the future of our families is serious business, taking things too seriously will only stifle our creativity and ability to accomplish things effortlessly and elegantly. So enjoy your journey as much as your destination!

AUTHOR BIOGRAPHY: Six Figure Coach, Kathy Hagenbuch is the creator of the Six Figure Success Series Programs for entrepreneurs and small business owners, including the 'Six Figure Success Team Builder Program', 'Create Six Figures by Putting Your Business on Autopilot' and 'Six Figure Communication'. Kathy can help you discover the exact income producing activities and low-to-no cost marketing strategies that will allow you to immediately find MORE TIME, make MORE MONEY while WORKING LESS and having MORE FUN. Get Kathy's free e-course 'Insider Secrets to Creating Six Figures and Beyond with your Success Team' by visiting www.SixFigureSuccessTeamSecrets.com. Feel free to contact Kathy by email via Kathy@SixFigureSuccessTeamSecrets.com, or by phone: (703) 327-2100

DEBBIE BORDELON

Monroe asked me to write a story for this book. It was a grand shock, because I never thought of myself as someone people want to meet. I pondered for days what to write, or even if I *should* write something. How to become the type of person that other people want to meet? Me? I asked myself, "Why do people want to meet you, Debbie? Do people really want to meet you?"

You see, I manage a cafeteria at a local University. I'm not a published author. I'm not a celebrity. I'm not the person I would have expected to see in a book like this.

I went back to Monroe and asked if him if he was sure about including me in the book. He answered, "Debbie! Yes! Don't you get it? I asked you to be a part of this book precisely because you are someone I want to meet. Because you are so cool! And I want you to share your story! I want to share how you ended up meeting me in the first place, and everything else that charms me about you."

Needless to say, I was flattered. And with flattery comes confidence. And with confidence comes inspiration. So I sat down to write.

After thinking about it, it became plain to me that people do come to meet me every day because I feed them. They are hungry, I provide food, and thus I am the type of person that they want to meet. But beyond that, I asked myself, "Why do people want to meet anyone?" The answer was fairly clear: people generally want to be with people who are like minded, open, and approachable.

I mentioned to my co-worker about this story I was asked to write, and told her that I hadn't even started writing. My boss was in the office when the conversation began, and I told her of my dilemma and asked for her advice. Immediately she started spurting out things for me to write about: how I volunteered for girl scouts, or about my bowling league that I have run for 14 years now, or how I send care packages regularly to Iraq — that might give you a clue regarding how I ended up becoming Monroe's friend.

My boss also mentioned my run for office last year and the admirable percentage of the votes I received. I appreciated her comments, and she did inspire me, but to be inspired was not my task — I had to actually write something in answer to the question, why? And how! The how was easy enough: I asked Monroe if he would help write the story with me, and he said yes. But the hard question that was asked was why.

That lead me back to my original answer... people love to eat. So I went back to my office to chat again with my boss, and the Director of Dining Services suddenly walked in, and right into the middle of our conversation. After giving her a brief run down of the whole story, starting off with the *who, what, where, when, and whys*, she started giving me her suggestions.

"Just start writing," she said. "Write anything you can. Things will make sense. Here I am talking to you, and obviously because you're someone I like and want to meet. People appreciate that you get back to them promptly, and that you never leave anyone hanging."

She told me that people appreciate my cheerful manner, and that every one can tell that I am always smiling, even when on the phone. It began to occur to me that smiling is indeed my number one asset. A smile, I soon began to realize, will attract more people than perhaps anything else you can do or say, whether in person, on the phone, or even through the written word.

In addition, being friendly is another of my best attributes; people want to be with people who are open and approachable. I love to have fun all the time. I once was told, "If anyone needs to know where the center of the action is, all they have to do is look for you." Wow, what a compliment!

I guess that is how you become a person that people want to meet: by smiling, being friendly, being cheerful, being responsible, by really making great efforts to help anyone you can, no matter what the trouble it may be to you. I do these things every day — not just three or four days a week, and not just when I feel like it: I do these things consistently and constantly. And I've found that people want to meet and know such a genuine person with such a reputation.

And since you might be wondering how I met Monroe and became the type of person *he* wanted to meet, I'll tell you that it started when I saw a classified ad that he took out in *Premiere Magazine* while he was in Iraq. His ad talked about how even though his dreams were on hold because of the war, he knew that with 'supporters like me', the dreams were not dead; just postponed. He had a photo of himself, and talked about his movie, *In the Wake*, and encouraged readers to sign up to his email lists, and to write to him in Iraq, and help him keep his dreams alive. Well... I did. And I became a huge fan of Monroe Mann. And I sent him care packages, and emails, and yes, signed up to all of his email lists. Monroe became my friend too, and in his words, even a fan of *me!* And when he got home from the war, he sent me signed copies of his books and his band's CD. And I in turn made great efforts to get his band's CDs distributed throughout my university, sent copies of his books to a friend of mine named Michael Essany (the host of the Michael Essany Show tv show), and I told Monroe that I was going to do everything I could to make him famous and successful in return for serving our country. True to my word, I couldn't say no when he asked me to write this story... even if it did take me a while to realize that I am somebody that other people want to meet.

P.S. A few weeks after I passed out Monroe's CDs to random kids at the school, and played *Running for Famous* songs on the stereo in the cafeteria, I heard the custodian whistling a tune while mopping the floors. Undeniably familiar, I asked him what song he was singing. "I don't know, but I can't get it out of my head! Some kids were playing it the other day, and I've been whistling it ever since." I walked away smiling, knowing that I was helping Monroe's ROMP band *Running for Famous* become the type of band that everyone in America would want to listen to. ROMP ON MONROE!

AUTHOR BIOGRAPHY: Debbie Bordelon is an Associate Manager at Valparaiso University, Valparaiso, IN and is currently working on a book entitled, *Adventures in Dining*.

debbiebordelon@aol.com

www.myspace.com/DebbieBordelon

GRAHAM GUERRA:
How I became the type of person Keith Ferrazzi wanted to meet

I am a fine-artist living and working in Brooklyn, New York… and even though a handful of family members, friends and colleagues consider me a "star," and I have indeed achieved a degree of success in the New York art world — you've probably never heard of Graham Guerra. [Editor's Note: I guess you just did.]

So, if you're among those who haven't heard of me, you're not alone… Keith Ferrazzi (author of *Never Eat Alone*) didn't know who I was at one point either.

Like many others who have read his superb book, *Never Eat Alone*, I was extremely impressed with his genuinely fresh approach to the crude and overused business term: "networking." Throughout the book he weaves his own brand of storytelling with practical advice to achieve brilliant distinction between coarse glad — handling and building sincere business relationships… ones based on generosity, not score keeping.

To say the least, though, Keith and I ran in very different circles. He was an established author and businessman; I was a young, hard-working curator, painter, and part-time professor. There wasn't much that I could offer him other than the possibility of a friendship — which even in my mind didn't seem very compelling. Nevertheless I was intent on meeting him so I developed a plan that I now know to have been guerrilla networking in action.

I began by learning as much as I could about Keith and was happy to discover that our backgrounds were similar and we shared many of the same interests. Most importantly, however, it turns out Keith and I have the same alma mater: Yale University. That's why I was understandably pleased when in October 2005 (shortly after his book was released), I received an invitation to hear him speak at a Yale University alumni meeting in Washington, DC. Not only did this provide me with a great opportunity to meet Keith, but I also hoped his generosity might extent to my mother, Mary Eule Scarborough.

She and her husband, David, had just completed writing their first draft of a business book. I'd read their manuscript and was pleasantly surprised by their ability to transform complex marketing concepts into a profoundly simple model. It was well written and practical, and yet comprehensive enough for more seasoned professionals. I thought they should look for a publisher, but they disagreed. They were first-time writers and the odds were stacked against them. There wasn't much of a chance that a reputable agent — let alone a publisher — would take that leap of faith.

Additionally, I was astute enough to recognize that I was not the most impartial evaluator and knew they needed candid and unbiased feedback from an objective source — preferably someone at the top of their field.

Enter: Keith Ferrazzi.

Undaunted by my lack of celebrity appeal, I emailed Keith. I asked his assistant if he might meet with us before his presentation and if he'd be willing to read the manuscript and offer any insights and advice he might have. It was a long shot and we weren't optimistic. Our cynical natures — mine inborn, my mom's due to spending one too many years in corporate America — assured us that we'd be lucky to get a reply, let alone 10 minutes of his time.

But the joke was on us because Keith was, and is, the "real deal." True to his business philosophy, generous spirit, and boundless energy, he agreed to meet with us — not for 10 minutes, but for more than an hour!

The result?

I am proud to say that Keith is my mentor and friend. Whenever he comes to New York, he invites me out to dinner with people he knows and likes... especially those interested in the arts. When I'm in California, we meet for coffee, dinner, or a grocery store visit (read the book, you'll understand.)

Even better, not long after I met Keith he invited my brother, Zach — a Navy aviator and film director who lives in San Diego — to a dinner party at his home in LA where he introduced him to some of his friends in the film industry (Check out Zach's website: www.InfidelisProductions.com). Later, Zach acted as the conduit for Keith and several other dignitaries to spend an amazing night aboard a naval aircraft carrier.

Moreover, Keith liked Mary and David's book, *The Procrastinator's Guide to Marketing* (Entrepreneur Press, November 2007) so much that he wrote the foreword!

My mom now continues the journey that Keith inspired. She's recently co-authored another book (*Mastering Online Marketing*, Entrepreneur Press, January 2008); her and David's small business consultancy and website are booming; and she's regularly invited to speak at seminars and conferences.

Here's how Keith humorously described our guerrilla networking in an email: *"Artist son, Graham, dragged mom to one of my talks in DC. They drove hours. Got introduced to son Zach a LT in the Navy. Graham is now starting a network of young artists and art investors in NY with my friend, Paul; and Zach and I are taking CEOs on carriers to show them that they should hire our sons and daughters when they finish serving our country. I'm introducing Zach (also a budding filmmaker) to my friends in the biz. Mom is still working on her marketing book and I'm introducing it to my publisher and using it to teach young marketers at Ferrazzi Greenlight. One big circle!"* And so it goes...

Unfortunately, many of us learn life's biggest lessons the hard way. I am no exception... most of my hard earned epiphanies resulted from disappointments. Gratefully, this time it was different and I learned several life-altering (and guerrilla networking) lessons without donating an ounce of my blood:

- Don't be afraid to reach out to others for help; even if those you contact are "out of your league" personally or professionally, the worst they can say is "no." At best, they just might want to meet you.

- ■ Audacity is a virtue... and may actually be the very trait that gets you noticed.

- ■ Time will either uphold you or expose you... and you'll meet the same people on the way down, as you did on the way up.

- ■ Regardless of your situation, you can enrich other people's lives by asking for, and offering, help when needed

Though you may not currently be in a position to reciprocate a favor from someone you ask help from, you will eventually find a way to repay their kindness, even if it is only shamelessly plugging their book. Did I mention Keith's book is, *Never Eat Alone*, and you should run — not walk — to your nearest book store and buy it, immediately? And did I mention that while you're there, you should pick up another copy of Monroe & Jay's book *Guerrilla Networking* for a friend?

AUTHOR BIOGRAPHY: Graham Day Guerra is one of New York's City's most promising contemporary artists and curators. He's earned rave reviews for his solo and group shows as well as his first curatorial effort, "The Hedonistic Imperative" which premiered in the city in 2005 and has since moved to Houston, TX. In addition to creating his own work in his studio in Brooklyn — where he lives — he is a part-time professor at one of the nation's premier art schools, Pratt Institute. Graham received his bachelor's degree from Rhode Island School of Design and earned a master's degree in fine arts from Yale University. If you'd like to find out more about him, visit his website at: www.grahamguerra.com.

347-365-2965

grahamguerra@aya.yale.edu

ASHLEY ANN SERAFIN

The most important guerrilla networking tactic in my opinion is a positive attitude. People do not always remember what you say, but in order to make an impact in someone's life you must make them feel something that they do not forget. I have lived my life knowing that time is precious and we must leave an impact on all those we come in contact with, and as a result, people tend to want to 'meet me' because of that.

For starters, at the tender age of 18 I worked as a receptionist for a company, and in that position, developed relationships with all those who called in through the switchboard. They not only wanted to meet me; they *had* to meet me. Being enthusiastic, even over the phone, set a tone for the people I spoke with. People enjoyed speaking to me because I shed light on their situation.

Meanwhile, a temp agency that the company had used heard I was leaving the firm and because my reputation had spread around the company, the temp agency representative told me to keep his contact information; to call him if I ever needed anything. I had become the type of person he thought his clients would want to meet.

I put his number in my purse thinking I would never need it; I already had a new job lined up. A month later, though, I needed his number — now he had become the type of person that I wanted to meet. I worked a few temporary positions and then came another one: I was asked to work just one week for a company answering their phones — strictly temporary.

Well, I went in that week, did more than was expected of me, and at the end of the week... I was asked to stay, part-time. As I worked part-time, though, I began developing relationships with (and trust among) our sales representatives and soon thereafter, I was bought out from the temp agency and hired as a full-time customer service representative. Progress! However, I was explicitly told that very rarely were there promotions in the company; it was not something they did often, and it was not something I should expect.

I was really happy, though, because I landed my first real full time job and was making a decent amount of money given that I had just graduated high school. Moreover, something I have always lived by was the idea that I should always strive to produce more than is expected of me. If I am making $10.00 an hour, I thought, I should be producing work as if I were making $20.00 an hour. By doing this, I would increase my value as an employee and as a person. I would become a valuable asset to the company. I would become someone who is always focused on finding a solution rather than focusing on the problem.

As a result, when customers would call in, they would often request to talk to me by name because of my understanding of what was best for them as well as the company. Our customers wanted to know that they were being listened to and — more importantly — understood, and because I gave that to customers, they wanted to work with me. Developing the skill of listening — truly listening —

to others is a valuable skill to have in everything you do. When you listen to others you are able to connect with their true needs; it's the only way you can truly learn how to assist them.

To further this end, I continued to develop myself — because that's what guerrilla networking is all about. I did things that I enjoyed doing and spent time with likeminded people. I looked at people I admired and emulated the skills that these successful people had. I took a look at the people in my life and spent more time with those who were an inspiration to me. I began reading time management books, going to seminars to further my business knowledge and going to classes to further my skills. It is not the company's responsibility to mold you into the employee they want. *You* must take it upon yourself to study and learn the necessary skills needed to remain a person who is in demand.

Go figure, about one year after working as an 'unpromotable' customer service representative, I was promoted. I was now the Sales and Marketing Coordinator (and all before the legal drinking age!)

I was sent around the country all expenses paid to represent our company. Along my journey I met some truly inspiring and influential artists such as Karen Neuburger (featured on Oprah's favorites), Joshua Greene (author of *Milton's Marilyn*), and many entrepreneurs. I was able to meet face to face with our sales representatives and customers, and in so doing, truly came to understand that our customers were real people; not just a voice on the other end of a phone. I began to realize that these customers are business owners with families and to do lists and problems and dreams, just like you and me. I began to realize that establishing these relationships was going to take a lot of time, and a plan.

As such, I needed to learn time management and how to prioritize a daily to-do list. No one was doing that for me. My new boss worked — literally — in a completely different state, and moreover, was on the road the majority of his time. I didn't really have someone looking over my shoulder anymore, and now needed to work my own day and take full responsibility for what needed to be done. In so doing, I became someone that customers could rely on. Whether it was my job to do it or not, I put people first. I went beyond my job description, and was soon recognized for that.

Within one year of that first unlikely promotion, I was promoted once again, this time to my current position of Customer Service Manager, at the age of 23. It was only two promotions ago that I was told by management that there were no full-time positions, and certainly no promotions. Within four years, though, I managed to turn a one-week temp job into a full-time career, and now I work with the top buyers in my industry.

To this day, I have never stopped learning. I continue to develop skills and constantly strive to live a life I love. I listen to empowering and motivational tapes while in the car and surround myself with a wonderful support system of friends and family. On my own time I read as many books as I can, go to seminars to learn anything from leadership to acting to investing. Knowledge is power, and because of that fact, I always make it a point to have something exciting to talk about whenever I meet people, no matter what their background.

It's become very clear to me: people want to meet someone who is confident, compassionate, and worthy of their respect.

Be that person — and more.

AUTHOR BIOGRAPHY: Ashley Ann Serafin is a manager within a leading stationery & craft wholesaler in New Jersey. She is also an actress in the New York City area and has performed on stage in productions such as Black Metropolis and has modeled for Joyce Leslie, Macy's, and Seventeen Magazine's prom issue. Ashley Ann is a graduate of Wayne Valley high school and continued studying at the NJ School of Dramatic Arts (with teachers such as Olinda Turturro) and Monroe Mann's Unstoppable Artists Business School in New York City. She spends some of her free time raising money for finding a cure for breast cancer.

She can reached be via ashleyannserafin@yahoo.com or via www.ashleyannserafin.com.

KNOX VANDERPOOL:
SAYiWON'T®

Our guerrilla networking campaign simply evolved from our logo and the concept itself: **SAYiWON'T®!** — the slogan on all of our t-shirts and apparel. The innate qualities of the wording, phrase, language, and power behind the concept all created its own Guerrilla Network, and people wanted to be a part of it.

Think about this: I can tell you all day what I think you *can* do or *will* do. I can lift you up and tell you exactly what you *want* and *need* to hear. But, if I tell you that you ***can't*** or ***won't*** succeed, then the conversation changes. It adds an emotional and motivational fuel to the fire. It fits the basic principle of our humanity. Is it fight or flight? And the bottom line throughout history is that all successful people *fight!*

Our brand and clothing line isn't challenging people in what they are trying to accomplish, but rather it is helping them answer the challenges that come with thinking outside the box and creating, pursuing, and accomplishing their own endeavors. *SAYiWON'T... and i will*®.

As we developed our business plan and began working events across the country, setting up our booth space, handing out promotions, or organizing after — parties, the guerrilla networking naturally happened. People wanted clothing with our concept on it. Initially, we were out meeting new people — everywhere — in person and online, but now they were out trying to meet us. The power behind our product and company really began to draw consumers and fans toward us. People were beginning to gravitate towards us and our products. It's really hard to wear **SAYiWON'T**® apparel and not have anyone energetically say, "You won't!" or "I will!" or "Where did you get that?" And the responses arose in the most random markets, and within markets that were seemingly unlikely to cross-over. As people began to notice **SAYiWON'T**® in all these different markets and began to understand the connections, the true identity of the concept began to grow — and the guerilla networking really surfaced.

For us, the truth is that guerrilla networking was never a term or a strategy we embraced or set out to achieve. But we quickly noticed its existence and claim as a viable tactic. With limited money and the desire to spread our brand as quickly as possible, we knew we had to get **SAYiWON'T**® in the right places and in the right spotlight.

Technically, we referred to what we were doing as "selling records" and creating "fans." The music industry displays the power of guerrilla networking better than any. Fans follow musicians for a number of reasons, but if any, the strongest reason is because of seemingly shared experiences — which ironically is what musicians are trying to achieve; to make the audience feel what you feel.

The same goes for **SAYiWON'T**®. We understand the human condition. Humans want to be successful, want to fulfill emotional needs, want to push the envelope, want to create, and want to answer challenges. **SAYiWON'T**® promotes the human condition and because the human condition promotes **SAYiWON'T®**, guerrilla networking has occurred naturally.

Guerrilla networking has allowed **SAYiWON'T®** to create fans. It has allowed us to establish a market that identifies with the brand and that wants to be a part of the concept. Our consumers are strong individuals — individuals with grit, sincerity, and a restless soul. They understand the concept. They want to be a part of the concept. They ALL answer any challenge with, " **SAYiWON'T®**." It's who they are or want to be, and they do it either because of the desire to be a part of a movement or because it's the natural response for an adventuresome individual. And by starting a movement based on a concept that brings out the best in one's self, we became a movement that other people wanted to be a part of.

Tell me that i can't do it.
Tell me that i shouldn't even try. Tell me
It's impossible. Tell me
The risk is too high, the challenge
Too much, or the feat
Too tough. Tell me that i won't do it
And i Will.
SAYiWON'T®

AUTHOR BIOGRAPHY: Knox Vanderpool is the CEO of SAYiWON'T®. A graduate of Phillips Exeter Academy in New

Hampshire and the University of the South in Tennessee, Vanderpool is a former collegiate athlete and coach.

cus@sayiwont.com

www.sayiwont.com

PAUL RIECKHOFF

My name is Paul Rieckhoff. I am an Iraq war combat veteran. I came back from the war in Iraq 2004, and worked diligently to become a prime mover and shaker behind a movement that educates people about the war in Iraq, and advocates on behalf of the veterans that served there. This grassroots organization soon blossomed into the Iraq & Afghanistan Veterans of America with offices in New York and Washington and over 60,000 members nationwide.

Things grew *very* quickly, and I was quickly asked to be interviewed by numerous major newspapers, magazines, and television talk shows ranging from *Hardball* with Chris Matthews to *The Charlie Rose Show* to *The Colbert Report*. I created a network of recognized Iraq war experts, and in 2005, I signed a book deal with Penguin Publishing for *Chasing Ghosts* — which just came out in paperback.

How did this all happen? I got behind a cause that I was passionate about — and to many other people as well — and built a network to take it national. I created a model that leveraged the positive energy of regular people, utilized the internet and created positive change for our country.

My fellow veterans and I worked hard to create a globally recognized organization that people are proud to be a part of.

AUTHOR BIOGRAPHY: Paul Rieckhoff, 32, is the Executive Director and Founder of Iraq and Afghanistan Veterans of America (IAVA), a non-partisan non-profit founded in 2004 with tens of thousands of members in all 50 US states. Rieckhoff was a First Lieutenant and infantry rifle platoon leader in the Iraq war from 2003 to 2004. He is now a nationally recognized authority on the war in Iraq and issues affecting troops, military families and veterans. Honored by *Esquire* magazine as one of "America's Best and Brightest" in 2004, Rieckhoff has appeared on hundreds of radio and television programs.

Recent appearances include: *ABC, The Charlie Rose Show, 60 Minutes, The NewsHour with Jim Lehrer, Paula Zahn Now, This Week With George Stephanopoulos, Good Morning America, Anderson Cooper 360, Countdown with Keith Olbermann, Hardball with Chris Mathews, The NBC Nightly News, ABC World News Tonight, The CBS Evening News, Hannity and Colmes, Big Story with John Gibson, BBC World, NPR's Morning Edition, All Things Considered, Fresh Air,* and *The Colbert Report.* He has been featured in *U.S. News and World Report, Newsweek, The New York Times, GIANT Magazine, Washington Post, L.A. Times, Army Times, Wall Street Journal, Reuters, The New York Post, Newsday* and *A.P.* Rieckhoff's first book, a critically acclaimed account of his experiences in Iraq and activism afterwards, entitled *Chasing Ghosts,* was published by Penguin in May 2006 (paperback published May 1, 2007).

info@IAVA.org

www.iava.org

www.chasingghosts.com

www.myspace/paulrieckhoff

BONES RODRIGUEZ

My name is Bones Rodriguez, and I became a guerrilla networker completely by accident; let me tell you the story...

As an actor, I was doing what I was taught to do — perform in little shows for my friends and family, doing crappy temp jobs just to pay the bills, and WAITING to be discovered and made into a millionaire.

Fortunately, I realized that it doesn't work like that.

I started reading as many books as I could on success, business and entrepreneurship, and found that CREATIVE THOUGHT was an overwhelming theme in overcoming obstacles and solving problems. I also joined an improv group which taught me about creative thought as a tool for acting.

These were new ideas to me, because in school I learned to do things as other people had done them — even in art classes we're taught how other people do things instead of learning to think for ourselves and CREATE.

I started applying the idea of creative thought to my life, and wrote out some of my goals (I add to the list all the time): I wanted to become an Actor, an Author, and an Entrepreneur.

So I ditched the crappy temp jobs and started several businesses, online and off. Most of them were failures, but as I learned from each failure, I learned to be even more creative, and a few started working and bringing me income.

Soon, I applied what I had learned from my failures in business to my acting career, and as a result, I booked my first commercial.

Then my second.

Then my third.

I kept booking commercial work (and still do), and soon people at parties started asking me how I was doing it, and how I managed to have an acting career without a day job.

This was the beginning of my becoming a guerrilla networker; people began seeking me out because I was doing something they valued.

My answers became an eBook: "No More Waiters — How to Build Your Acting Business WITHOUT a Day Job" (www.NoMoreWaiters.com). I also wrote a version for non-actors called "The Beep-Beep System" (www.BeepBeepSystem.com).

These eBooks helped people THINK CREATIVELY and design businesses they could start related to their hobbies. Again, people were seeking me out because I was doing something they valued.

One day I took my own advice and paired my love for *Star Trek* with my love for the opposite sex, and came up with the idea for my book *Captain Kirk's Guide To Women — How to Romance Any Woman In The Galaxy*. Even though every book I read said it would take at least two years, I attracted an agent within a week by using one of the ideas I had learned from one of my failed businesses.

When Simon and Schuster saw all I had done up until this point (they especially liked how I proposed to my wife on YouTube), they signed a contract with me to write the book.

How did it happen? Simple: They liked the idea. It was the type of idea *they* wanted to publish.

Remember, this all happened accidentally. All I did was make the effort to become the person I wanted to become all along, and go figure, there were people at every turn who had been looking for just that person — lucky me!

I was even more surprised when Monroe Mann told me that he and Jay Conrad Levinson wanted a story from me for their book. I hadn't thought of myself as a "guerilla networker"; rather, just as someone who was using CREATIVE THOUGHT to become someone unique and special, and who was helping whomever I could along the way. I was truly honored to be asked to write something for this book.

Do you know why?

Because Monroe Mann and Jay Conrad Levinson are Guerrilla Networkers.

They ATTRACT people around them by using their CREATIVE THOUGHT to help people.

When YOU start helping people with your own creative skills (we all have them), YOU'LL be who THEY want to meet too.

In fact, I want to meet you just because you're reading this book; It proves to me that you are developing your own creative problem-solving mind, and I am attracted to people like that — but isn't everyone?

So how do you become the type of person others want to meet? THINK CREATIVELY about how to solve problems, publicize it, and they will find you.

Send me an email: Bones@BonesRodriguez.com, I'd love to hear what you come up with!

AUTHOR BIOGRAPHY: Bones Rodriguez is an Actor, Author, and Entrepreneur from New York City. Yes, you've seen him. His videos, books, and many other projects can be found by visiting www.BonesRodriguez.com.

DENNIS HURLEY

My name is Dennis Hurley. I'm an actor in New York City. As actors often do, I submitted to audition for a movie, and in particular for the part of Silas in Ron Howard's *The DaVinci Code*, a role very specific to my type, "Albino." Since there are only 17,000 albinos in this country, I figured there couldn't be all that many albinos who were also male and also actors: I was truly perfectly niched for this role. Truly, how many male actors would be fighting for the role as much as I would be? I was driven to get this part.

Well, the casting company wrote me back to inform me that they were going *a different way*. Turns out they wanted "a name". So Ron cast Paul Bettany, a non-albino. And they bleached his hair and painted his skin white.

Great! But I didn't get mad. I got even.

You see, while yes, I'm an actor first and foremost, I am also a screen writer. Well, one night, after reading Dan Brown's novel again, I found some material in there — particularly the parts involving Silas — that would make great material for a fun parody! So instead of getting frustrated with not being cast and just DOING THE SAME THING, i.e. submitting for other films — *trying to meet people* — I decided to write and produce a short parody of *The Da Vinci Code*, and release it on the Internet at the same time *The Da Vinci Code* was to be released in theaters.

The Result?

Dennis Hurley and *The Albino Code* were Featured on *CNN*, *MSNBC, The Insider, ET, FOX NEWS, Inside Edition, Good Morning America* and in *The Boston Herald, The New York Post, The Metro, The Philadelphia Inquirer, The Toronto Star,* and *People Magazine.* It was screened at Boston Film Night at the Regent Theatre in Boston, MA, The Sedgwick Theater in Mt. Airy, PA, Open Screen at the Coolidge Corner Theatre, Brookline, MA, The Drama Book Shop, Inc., Bar Nine in New York City, and Online @ www.haydenfilms.com, care of the Pacific Palisades Film Festival in Pacific Palisades, CA. The website crashed in its first week.

And since that time? You guessed it: I've received offers to write and act in double the number of projects that I had SUBMITTED to before the film's release.

****People wanted to meet me!****

AUTHOR BIOGRAPHY: Dennis Hurley is writer/executive producer/star of the internationally acclaimed comedy, *The Albino Code*, a short spoof of *The Da Vinci Code*, which can be found at www.albinocode.com. Dennis is originally from Hingham, Massachusetts. He holds a B.F.A. in Acting from Ithaca College and studied with the Upright Citizens Brigade Theatre in New York City. He also co-founded Down Cellar Films in 2005. Dennis' recent work includes a deleted scene from *Running With Scissors* (Tri-Star) starring Gwyneth Paltrow and Annette Benning, as well as work on *Law & Order*, *Sex & the City*, *The Manchurian Candidate*, & *Saturday Night Live*. He is also a member of ImprovBoston and The Tribe Theatre in Boston's Theatre District, and is a client/student of Unstoppable Artists. More information about Dennis is available at www.dennis-hurley.com. To contact him, send an email to: downcellar@gmail.com.

www.MrsCrowling.com
www.BostonAwards.com
www.dennis-hurley.com
www.albinocode.com
www.sawyerandhurley.com

PHIL MALANDRINO

When Monroe and Jay asked, "How did I become someone that others wanted to meet," I took a long hard look at how I became the person that I have become: the owner of a multi-million dollar photocopier sales, service, and repair business in Manhattan called Photo Dynamics. It didn't take long to realize that it was a hard question to answer. Certainly not in a word or two.

After some thought, however, I realized that over time I had been very careful about who I chose to associate with, and what I became known for. I realized that a reputation is carefully constructed over time, and not something to consider lightly.

To that end, it has always been important to me not to tarnish the trust I've earned from others. I have always given 100% to any task with nothing less than success in mind. It has become known that when Phil Malandrino is involved in any project, that project will be hard work, interesting, educational, fun, successful, and a source of mutual inspiration. All of this creates "the legend" status that I have become recognized for. This is the true source of the interest to meet and/or work with me: people trust that anything I am involved with is going to be successful for all and rewarding to them.

Moreover, although I am an accessible individual, full access is only granted to those who have the same goals in mind. Also, full access has always been denied to people with manipulative intentions, ill will, or negative energy emitted towards me or to others. I truly believe that my energy is fueled by the positive individuals I surround myself with.

So why do people want to meet me? First, I became known as a person of honor and integrity, as someone who can be trusted, and as someone with a sense of humor. In addition, I work really hard, right along side those people who I have given the opportunity to work with me. Next, I am a source of positive energy, and my attitude helps generate the energy that others need to fuel *their* drive. Most importantly, I always feel the need to live up to others' expectations of me. This maintains "the legend" which is so important to my reputation.

In conclusion, I guess the answer to the question is: my reputation.

AUTHOR BIOGRAPHY: Phil Malandrino is the owner/founder of Photo Dynamics, a photocopy sales and service company located in Chelsea, Manhattan, and is the author of an upcoming book about how to buy the perfect copier for your business. Phil appears as the Japanese Judge in the comedy film, *Origami Deathmatch*, and is developing a number of film projects of his own. Phil is also a student/client of Unstoppable Artists. He can be reached via phil@philmalandrino.com and www.philmalandrino.com.

DOUGLAS C. WILLIAMS

After reading *Guerrilla Marketing* on Monroe's recommendation and taking his business course for artists, I decided to launch a publicity stunt for one of my current projects at the time. My new musical *Windows of Lucidity* was about to debut in NYC and I wanted to somehow obtain national exposure. My stunt was to break the Guinness World Record for an Individual Singing Marathon.

I was going to sing for more than 25 hours straight to promote myself and my new show. I was faced with a very limited budget and timeframe.

But my idea was unique, exciting, and so much fun that I didn't really have to ask for help. People volunteered their services and support just because they wanted to be a part of something cool.

I was given permission to sing in front of The Museum of Natural History, which is very rare. I even obtained sponsors and organizers for the event from just a few press releases and word of mouth.

Immediately following the event, NBC sent a limo to deliver me to *The Carson Daly Show* studios where I made my national TV debut and plugged myself, my event, and my new show to the whole country! Needless to say, the show did very well.

I even had the distinct privilege of singing a song on national television.

The best part: I didn't find the connections to make all of this possible. They all found me. I became the type of person they wanted to meet.

AUTHOR BIOGRAPHY: Douglas C. Williams is an actor/writer/producer living in Manhattan, and the CEO of Three Feet From Gold Productions. He is also a client/student of Unstoppable Artists.

douglas@douglascwilliams.com
www.douglascwilliams.com

ROBERTA MUSA

When Monroe asked me the question — "How did you become the type of person other people wanted to meet?" — I didn't immediately know the answer. While I did successfully win an election (twice) to public office as part of the Maine State Legislature, I felt that my winning the election went beyond just the issues. I began asking my fellow politicians and teachers what their thoughts were, asking them, "Why do you interact with me, and work with me?"

At the end of my investigation, I tallied up the results and came to four conclusions. I suspect that others connect with me because of...

a) *An inviting demeanor.* People frequently go out of their way to tell me "You are always smiling." I take that as a complement and a commentary on why some are initially attracted to me. Many go a step further and comment on my eyes. Apparently I am looking at them in a way that they find welcoming and open; in a way that lets them know that I am focused on them and listening to what they are saying — which is usually true.

b) *A calm and calming appearance.* I suspect that some people invite me into their world because I am naturally quiet and rarely get flustered or overly emotional. People who are consciously or subconsciously seeking a balancing presence seem to gravitate towards me, especially those at the emotional extremes.

c) *A slowness to decision/reaction.* On a mental level, I am a global thinker. It takes me a long time to come to an opinion/conclusion on an issue because my mind demands to consider every issue's many facets and has the ability to tolerate a lot of ambiguity before coming to a conclusion. While this may be seen as a weakness, it may be a strength in working with others who perceive it as openness (which I hope it is!)

d) *My personal knowledge and skills.* I believe many people seek me out because they value my opinion in areas where I have particular expertise or skill.

What I did find interesting is that the very attributes that some people found appealing could be off-putting to others. For instance, calmness can be considered reticence or haughtiness; slowness to decision can be taken as stupidity or timidity; etc. I guess that's why "there is someone for everyone" and why my best guerrilla networking advice for you is to be yourself, but be your *best* self, i.e. discover your talents, and develop them to the utmost.

AUTHOR BIOGRAPHY: Roberta Muse is an elected member of the Maine State Legislature, and a French teacher at Fryeburg Academy, in Fryeburg, Maine. She can be reached via robertamuse@gmail.com and www.muses.org

KIP GIENAU:
The Illusionist

"I was told by three different people that I had to meet you!"

Why do people constantly say this about me? It is partly because of these techniques that I have become what many consider *'the master illusionist.* I move through the crowds and *appear* to be everywhere at once. I appear to know everyone at every event I attend — and I attend a lot of events — and everyone *thinks* they know me.

The strategy I use is based on the fact that when there's a celebrity in the house, word spreads like wildfire. Since everyone wants to know the popular individual... I simply become popular.

You see, an illusionist can make people see things that aren't there, make other things disappear, and make himself appear to be in many places at the same time. Yes, in that regard, I am an illusionist. And, it is why I am so successful at networking. Another associate remarked about me recently, "Kip, you embody the true meaning of networking." And that comment alone made me realize that I am indeed someone that others want to meet.

By employing guerrilla networking techniques, you too can become the person everyone wants to meet, and people will as a result come up to *you*. You too can become a master illusionist. Sure, it will take some time and effort on your part, but it *will* pay off down the road when it seems like everyone is beating down your door. You will be more popular than Harry Houdini and, in keeping with Guerrilla Marketing techniques, it won't cost you a dime. Let me give you an example of what I mean.

Recently, I attended an event at the Coast Guard Academy in New London, Connecticut. There were over 160 people in attendance. Prior to the first speech, I managed to speak to over 80 attendees. How so?

First, I introduced myself to a small group gathered in one spot. We chatted. I remembered their names and learned a few things about each individual. Then I excused myself for a moment and met another individual, conversed, and then asked that person to meet some friends and introduced this new person to the people in the first group. I assisted in the introductions. Once conversation was flowing, I casually slipped away and found another individual. Before long 14 people were gathered around me. In time, I slipped away again and wandered off and started another group and so on.

To the casual observer standing on a balcony, it might have seemed that I was everywhere at once. By the time the evening ended, people were looking for me! They wanted to meet me and speak to me in more depth because, obviously, I must be someone important — how else would I have known everyone at the party?

Anyone can become the "go to" person if you are willing to let yourself go. Don't hold back and don't worry about what others think. Guerrilla networking is fun! Just don't expect immediate gratification. Think of it as a long term project — a continuous one where your goal is to develop strong and lasting relationships. People will always do business (when they are ready) with others they trust, admire, like, and respect. So, don't waste your money chasing customers. Spend a little time and energy inventing creative ways to make people come to you. If you apply this advice, then you too, will become a world class guerrilla networking expert. Yes, you too can become a master illusionist — and everyone will want to know you!

Before I sign off, here are some of the reasons I have become the person everyone wants to know — why I am the one person they think of whenever they need marketing advice. Each of these tactics will help *you* to become the type of person that everyone else wants to meet as well.

1. **Attend business events several nights each week.**

2. **Meet and Greet EVERYONE you see.**

3. **Focus on the people you meet.**

4. **Listen. Listen. Listen.**

5. **Exude enthusiasm.**

6. **Be fearless.**

AUTHOR BIOGRAPHY: Kip Gienau is the owner of Advertising Works CT, LLC, based in Waterford, CT, www.adworksct.com. He has been in the advertising industry for over 12 years, three as a Certified Guerrilla Marketing Coach. Kip's greatest strengths are networking and motivational speaking. His goal is to have happy, satisfied customers. He accomplishes that with his contagiously infective positive attitude and his enthusiasm for GM techniques. Gienau was recently selected as one of 30 world class Guerrilla coaches to contribute a chapter in Jay Conrad Levinson's new book, *Guerrilla Marketing on the Front Lines*.

Contact Information:
Phone: (800) 443-0667
Fax: (860) 443-0668
Kip@adworksct.com
www.adworksct.com

MARCIA HARP

I'd like to share a few very quick and simple guerrilla networking stories with you.

Two days ago, when teaching my acting and singing class, the owner of the school *came straight up to me* and couldn't say enough fabulous things about my singing performance the previous night. She never knew I could sing so well, and it was my voice that brought her up to me! Now she is writing up a cover letter — voluntarily mind you — to send to all the agents she thinks I'd be right for and is including my picture and resume with her stamp of approval.

She then told me that the students who performed in the acting category (my students) were some of the best she had ever seen. Beyond that, all the agents told her that my students are the best they've ever seen at her talent searches, and the owner said to me, "Marcia, you have raised my school up to a whole other level and at this point, you are simply not replaceable." Being irreplaceable is certainly a guerrilla networking principle. She now wants to promote my new show to support and further promote me as a performer and my one woman show.

Then, last night, nine of my students invited me to be honored at a banquet for the College Honor Society. *Each* could have taken a teacher of their own...but they *all* selected ME. I was honored!

But it didn't make any sense. Why just me? I asked them, "Why did you all select me? Why did you want to honor me? Why did you want to be with me?"

I loved their response.

"Because you are the best teacher ever! Because you care! Because you show us love!"

On the awards certificate itself was the following message: "Thank you for being a person who is inspiring and always motivating."

I guess this is why these same students continue to bring more and more of their friends to take my class. I had simply become the teacher their friends 'needed' to learn from.

And I guess all those years of developing my voice, the years of persistence and discipline, and the belief in myself and in my talents that I never allowed to falter, and then finally displaying it to the right people... it all paid off: I had become the type of singer people wanted to meet.

AUTHOR BIOGRAPHY: Marcia Harp is the star of the acclaimed one-woman show, *Where Was I When I Needed Me?*, and also the upcoming book of the same title. A former radio show host, she holds a BS Degree in Dance — Physical Education and Theatre Arts from Ohio State University and a Master of Arts Degree in Creative Arts from San Francisco State University. As a world champion athlete, she set 10 world records at the 1998 AAU Power Lifting competition. She is also a student/client of Unstoppable Artists. She can reached via marcia@marciaharp.com and www.marciaharp.com.

SCOTT DUPONT:
Guerrilla Networker & Fund Raiser

Guerrilla networking is becoming the type of person other people want to meet. Well, people often come up to me asking how I am able to raise money for my film, video, and DVD projects — which is a very tough task as you have to disclose to potential investors that they could possibly lose all of their money!

The story I always share to answer that question focuses on how I met my last Executive Producer (Jeff Deane) while doing extra work on Adam Sandler's film *"The Waterboy"*. The following story is how I had become someone that a person like Jeff Deane would eventually want to meet (and give money to).

On the day of shooting, my good friend and actress Kristi Moore and I arrived early in the morning and were herded like cattle into bleachers at a large football stadium. Kristi and I ended up sitting next to this older guy in his 40s with a HUGE sombrero hat and an old t-shirt. Sometimes I really wonder who are the serious actors, who are aspiring actors doing extra work, who is there to glimpse their favorite celebrity actor, or who is just showing up for the free meals.

Now I must admit Jeff could have fallen into the final category, but as a Guerrilla Networker, I try and never judge anybody until after I really get to know the person. So, I decided to strike up a conversation with Jeff. He turned out to be a really down to earth guy who had been on a few other movie sets over the years and was really passionate about the film business and just did extra work here and there as a hobby.

Well, during our conversation, it turned out he had gone to Rollins College, where not only I too had attended school, but also where our director had also attended. Already I was becoming the type of person Jeff wanted to meet (and at this point, I still didn't know that Jeff was in a position to finance my film.)

So we talked. Since Rollins is a small liberal arts college in Winter Park, Florida, we ended up having a few friends in common. Later on in the day, I told him that my director friend and I had produced a really funny, award winning short film called *"The Brothers"* and that we were going to make it into a feature. I did not ask him for any money upfront — because I didn't know he had any — but simply spoke about all the success the short film had by winning film festivals all over the country and how it played so well to audiences. After our day of extra work, Jeff and I kept in touch with one another, and I eventually sent him a copy of the short film. He watched, got really excited himself, and a few weeks later — ta da! — he came on board as an investor with $10,000.

As the development and pre-production phases of the film advanced and Jeff got more involved with the project, we became close friends and he — ta da! — ended up investing quite a bit more money — well over half a million dollars to be precise — and became our main Executive Producer!

People ask me how I got Jeff to invest in the movie and I think it is because I had really studied the business for many years and we had a really talented team including our Director and fellow producers who had over 25 years combined experience in the business. And that put Jeff at ease. That made my production team the type of team that Jeff wanted to put his money behind. When you have a professional team with a track record and you have genuine passion for a project, that combination will ultimately attract investors. In the end, though, Jeff sold himself: he learned we had an exciting project on our hands, found out we had done our homework, and he wanted to be part of it. I laid out exactly what we wanted from an Executive Producer and Jeff was able to become part of our established production team, so the Guerilla Networking in fact cut both ways.

This second story (containing another valuable Guerilla Networking lesson) is about a friend of mine named Jack Murray, who was head of Prince tennis rackets and who later ran Wilson Sporting Goods, to name just a few of his successful business ventures. If you looked up 'successful businessman' in the dictionary, you would probably find Jack Murray's photo there smiling back at you.

Mr. Murray was one of my neighbors down in Florida and I became good friends with him over the years and always enjoyed being around him and learning whatever I could about business from him. My first business venture which I started with my best friend John Bridges was a chain of retail stores selling pre-paid phone cards back in 1993. We were the first retail store in the United States dedicated to selling these new "debit" phone cards and we had done our research and were just about to launch a mail order business and open up a few "pilot" stores in Florida.

At the time, Jack was up at his summer home in Princeton, New Jersey and I had arranged a meeting with him to secure at least $100,000 in financing. The market was about to explode, and Mr. Murray knew it. He was aware of the market growth through his good friend Charlie Brown (the CEO of AT&T at the time.)

Based on this, my partner John and I figured we had a slam dunk... plus the fact that we were all neighbors and friends. John & I ended up having a great meeting with Mr. Murray, and both John & I thought we were going to walk out with a check that very day. But at the end of the meeting, Jack turned to us and said: "I could easily write a check today and invest in your company, but I am not going to. Instead, I am going to give you some good advice which I think will help you boys." He explained, "You need to talk to people who are interested and excited about your business. I have no interest in telecommunications or these phone cards. I am passionate about sports and real estate. That is what gets me excited and where I ultimately invest my money."

While John and I walked out of that meeting totally crushed, that was probably the BEST business advice I have ever received in my life. We used it immediately, and only a few weeks later (after approaching people in the telecom industry and some of our early customers), we had almost $80,000.00 in start up capital for our business!

I continue to use that advice to this day with all of my film projects: do NOT assume that rich people are going invest in your business venture. You have 100 times a better a chance of getting people with less money but more interest and excitement in your business to invest than a really wealthy individual who does not share your passion. To date, most of my film investors have been aspiring actors or individuals who have a keen interest in the entertainment industry.

In the end, John and I had become the type of people that Jack Murray wanted to meet with, and he helped us become the type of people other people wanted to invest in. He gave John and I the greatest compliment that day by saying, "You kids (we were in our 20s then) remind of me when I was starting out in business."

AUTHOR BIOGRAPHY: Scott duPont is an award-winning actor who has appeared in over 50 films and over 100 commercials over the past 10 years. As a producer, Scott has raised over $1 million dollars and has produced over a dozen film, video, and tv projects including: *"The BROS."* just released by Lionsgate and is development on a new feature film titled: *"Ticket Trouble."*

duPont has been a board member of the Florida Motion Picture & Television Association (FMPTA) for the past 7 years and last year was elected as State President of the 34 year old trade association. Scott also served on the Board of Film Florida, and as past Chairman of the Florida Alliance of Media & Entertainment. Scott received the R. John Hugh Award for excellence and professionalism in the entertainment industry and was also awarded the "Up and Comers"

Award by the Orlando Business Journal and most recently was elected President of the Florida Cast & Crew Association. Scott also writes regular columns for *ChART Magazine* and *The Director's Chair*. For an agent that represents Scott in your area call (407) 629 - SCOTT. You can contact him directly via: ScottduP@juno.com and www.scottdupont.com.

KOLIE CRUTCHER:
Who Wouldn't Want to Meet Kolie Crutcher?

Back in 2005, I attended a "networking" event where representatives from different companies within the energy industry could meet one another. Before the event, we were all encouraged to bring our business cards so that we could network and brush shoulders with important people in the industry. Being young and relatively new to the company, it was explained to me that this event was a "must". So of course, I attended — all dressed up and with pockets full of business cards.

However, at the end of the event, I had a bunch of business cards from people I could not remember, and I felt exhausted from all the meaningless small talk. I thought to myself, "What a waste of time and energy! I really could have been doing something else to meet people."

Well, that was back in 2005. I didn't know it at the time, but that 'something else' I felt I could have been doing is exactly what I am doing now — guerrilla networking!

My name is Kolie E. Crutcher III, and I am the author of *Electric Living — The Powerful Life!* My good friend, mentor, and business associate Monroe Mann once told me that a published book is the ultimate marketing tool. He was right on target!

The whole process of writing and publishing *Electric Living* is a testament to the power of guerrilla networking — with every step, I was becoming more and more the type of person other people wanted to meet. For starters, a published book is the ultimate marketing tool, and the fact that I am publishing *Electric Living* says so many things about Kolie Crutcher. Four things that come to mind:

It says "Kolie Crutcher has credibility."

It says "Kolie Crutcher is an expert."

It says "Kolie Crutcher is thorough."

It says "Kolie Crutcher is intelligent."

Now who wouldn't want to meet a credible expert who is thorough and intelligent? Who wouldn't want to meet Kolie Crutcher?

Yes, every day, Kolie Crutcher is becoming the type of person others want to meet. How can I tell? Here are some of the things people have said to and about me recently:

- "Hey Kolie, we know you're probably busy right now, but a bunch of us were here talking about your book. When is it coming out? Can we come to your book signing party? Can we bring other people too?"

- "Kolie, someone told me that you are an actor too. Wow! An actor, engineer, and published author. I was telling my mom about you. She wants to come and see your play."

- "Kolie always seems to be doing something. I can't quite figure out what it is, but it seems like he has so much more going on than just his day job. The guy is like Clark Kent."

- "That's him! That's Kolie! That's the guy who wrote the book... Excuse me, are you really Kolie Crutcher. I mean you really look like him, but I wasn't sure."

- "Like I said, in this world, it's all about who you know. And I'm good because I know Kolie Crutcher."

Beyond this, an investor in Florida has just recently expressed great interest in helping finance my new venture entitled, *Get Money Magazine*, even though I never pitched him on it. He heard about it from some other people through the grapevine. Two up-and-coming rappers and a beauty contestant model have asked me to manage them, even though I have never advertised myself as a "talent manager". From just recently concluding my first public speaking engagement at a high school, to being requested to chaperone a group of Japanese businessmen through New York, Kolie Crutcher is rapidly becoming a person others want to meet and associate themselves with.

And this is just the beginning.

Think about this:

When you are not the type of person others want to meet, you give off this vibe of "Please, please talk to me. I'm really not worthy of your time, but since I admire you so much, I deserve it." What a groupie! When you are the type of person others want to meet, you give off this vibe of, "I'm important. What I have to offer will benefit YOU!"

Here's the bottom line: No matter what industry you yourself may be in, spend your time becoming the type of person others want to meet instead of always trying to meet others. Stop — pardon my speech — whoring yourself to your industry. Instead, invest some time and some effort and some serious thought into figuring out how you can stand out from the crowd. Sure, there's nothing wrong with wanting to meet other people who can help your career, but life is not a one way street. Other people have to want to meet you too!

AUTHOR BIOGRAPHY: Kolie E. Crutcher III is a recent graduate of the American Academy of Dramatic Arts in Manhattan. Working as an electrical engineer for Con Edison during the day, Kolie has combined his technical expertise with a unique flair of motivation in his first book entitled *Electric Living — The Powerful Life!* available August 2007. In addition to this ground-breaking motivational book, Kolie is finishing up his second book, *Diamondz in Da Ruff*, available early 2008. To accompany these projects, Kolie is working in collaboration with Brooklyn rapper MYNORiTY to release a motivational rap song that will be felt from the board room to the block. Other Kolie Crutcher ventures include *Get Money Magazine* — the online magazine of choice, *PIMP* (Person Imposing Mental Power) *Wear* — the urban clothing line, and *The Edison Files* — the sci-fi thriller movie. Kolie Crutcher (also a student/client of Unstoppable Artists) is a native of Memphis, TN, but currently resides in the Bronx, NY.

KolieCrutcher@ElectricLiving.net

www.ElectricLiving.net

ED SMITH

My approach to guerrilla networking has been to focus on my strengths and play off of them. Since I am a motivational expert with an extensive background in that area, I used this knowledge base to write a book that focused on success techniques, but with my own spin, which is fast results.

To that end, the book contains a series of quick tips you can use to move your life ahead RIGHT NOW. The title says it all: *60 Seconds To Success*.

A side benefit of keeping the book very simple and fast and devoid of "feel good" stories is that the book is huge overseas. Overseas they don't understand our local customs, etc, but do get the concepts. Also, since few people from the USA are known overseas, I am considered on equal footing with the big names from here. I jokingly describe my book as the only international best seller with less than 100 complete sentences.

Prior to writing the book, I had been the host of my own radio show for five years, called the Bright Moment show, but lost it. At that point I got a small cable TV show on Time Warner with the same name and theme (interviews with experts related to peak performance) and also containing the One Minute Motivator (a quick peak performance tip).

The radio show and the cable TV show allowed me to build my own knowledge in the area plus build a huge network of people working in the "success" area. Because all motivational speakers and authors were looking for publicity, I have gotten to know many of the top names in the "success" area such as Jack Canfield, Mark Victor Hansen , Brian Tracy, Les Brown, etc. — by having them on my shows. My shows provided me a classy way to network with them, and get testimonials and endorsements from them. It has also lead to somewhat related things like hosting other tv shows, teaching, and freelance writing assignments. The radio and tv shows helped me to become someone that other — more prominent people — wanted to meet.

In a crowded field, the more you have to show that you are credible, the more opportunities will come your way simply as a matter of course.

One thing has really helped my credibility is the use of the One Minute Motivators, because they have been a real success. I send them out daily, for free, via email; I use them on my Internet radio show and also on my cable TV show. Now in addition to keeping and expanding this fan base, I have now also expanded onto YouTube.com, by making video versions of the One Minute Motivator and posting them up. All of these activities tie back to each other and feed sales of the book, seminars, overseas book deals, etc.

In fact, these activities have even allowed me to promote my *wife's* practice as a Business and Life Coach. I quote Theresa A Smith, Business and Life Coach in the articles I write, I have her as my co-host on the TV show, I include her in my speaking engagements, and use free coaching sessions as a tie in promotion for book sales. So we build each other's business, while building our own business. And my mentioning her here in this book helps to make her someone YOU may want to meet.

So, what motivates me to keep pushing the envelope in looking for new ways to promote my work and encourage people to meet me? A number of years ago, the Internet put me out of business. At that time I vowed that I would never be caught out of date with technology again and I vowed to use it to bring my strengths into play. So I am constantly scanning the horizon for what is up and coming in the technology area. I must confess, though, that I don't always get it together. For instance, right now, I am trying to figure out how to mount my rabbit ears on my plasma TV.

Bottom line, prior to putting my guerrilla networking strategies into place, if you googled Edward Smith, the captain of the Titanic would be the only person to come up. Now if you google Edward W. Smith, I come up number one.

AUTHOR BIOGRAPHY: Edward W. Smith is the author of 60 Seconds To Success, the Producer/Host of the Bright Moment cable TV and internet radio show, President of the Bright Moment Seminars, is a motivational speaker and publishes the free, daily One Minute Motivator via email and youtube.com. He can be reached via edsmith@brightmoment.com and www.brightmoment.com.

SCOTT NORMAN

When I moved to Michigan, in order to help me get acclimated to the area (to make connections, find work, and so forth), I joined an alumni association for people who had — like myself — taught in Japan. Unfortunately, the group was suffering from a certain amount of apathy. People were spread out across the state, it was difficult to get everyone together, and the leadership had grown tired and unenthusiastic.

So, I took charge. I made a point of calling the president regularly and asking for meetings, which she arranged. I then volunteered to create a website and revamp their mailing list, which got my name in front of the membership. I was soon being asked to represent the chapter at national conferences. By the time elections were held later in the year (which I also helped to organize), I was the one elected president.

Suddenly, *I* was the one getting calls — from headhunters and employers who wanted access to the membership, from members who were looking for ways to contribute to the group, and from representatives from other chapters who wanted to pay me to develop their websites. People were reaching out to me, instead of the other way around.

A couple of years later, I was working on the set of *InZer0*, a local made-for-TV sci-fi film series shot entirely in Detroit. The premise for the project was that they would shoot, edit, and screen one episode a month, every month, for a year, to develop their filmmaking skills so that by the end of the year, they would be better filmmakers and have a great reel to show for it. It was a highly ambitious project, and it attracted a large cast and crew. All kinds of talent came out of the woodwork, from bad to great, many of whom were simply hooked on the idea of becoming famous due to their exposure in this project. They loved to just sit around chatting and gossiping about fame and fortune.

I didn't participate in this. I didn't reach out to a lot of people because it was difficult to tell who was serious or not. While I did socialize with my scene mates and others on the set, I spent most of my time running lines, visiting the set to be comfortable with the space, or quietly meditating — things to make my performance stronger.

From what others tell me, I did indeed shine on set and on screen. And apparently the word got out that I was a serious actor, because as the year went on, other filmmakers on the project were offering me roles in their projects. At the wrap party at the end of the year, people I had never seen or worked with directly were now making a point of introducing themselves to me and complimenting me on my work. They were coming up to *me*.

In both situations, all I did was focus on doing those things that would make me more interesting, more prepared, more desirable. I became the type of person other people wanted to meet.

AUTHOR BIOGRAPHY: After spending five years teaching English in Japan, and learning the importance of laughter in education, Scott V. Norman returned to his native New York City to train as an actor. Scott is now a professional actor, film producer, and a corporate trainer, bringing both dramatic and comedic characters to life on stage and film, and using comedy to enliven presentations on otherwise boring subjects. He is currently writing a book introducing Apple computers to pre-beginners. Scott is a client/student of Unstoppable Artists, and welcomes contact by email at Guerrilla@ScottVNorman.com, or via his website, www.ScottVNorman.com.

PETER BIELAGUS:
Connecting on a Whole Other Level

Shortly after I watched the last of my book advance money dwindle away — but shortly before I began my career as a professional speaker — I found myself jumping temporarily back into the financial world to bridge the income gap between the book advance and the soon to arrive speaking checks.

At the time, I landed in the red hot market of real estate closings, a typically dull but reliable industry that was enjoying double digit growth because of plummeting interest rates. My job was pretty much a sales job. I would approach real estate agents and mortgage brokers and ask them to send me their next deal so my company could handle the real estate closing.

There's a saying in sales that from 10 to 4 you're out the door. And so I was. I spent my days driving around in my territory, entering offices, and trying to fight my way through receptionists and managerial gatekeepers in order to get some face time in front of the people who could actually send me business.

While the market was red hot and while there was plenty of business out there, there were also plenty of other salespeople, just like me, fighting for that business. I tried my best to be generous and creative. At times I would spring for a dozen donuts and a jug of coffee and enter an office only to find *three* other sales people 'just like me' had already left their coffee and donuts. It soon dawned on me that some of the less-than-pleasant receptionists were that way simply because I was the 8th or 9th salesperson who had walked into the office that day.

It started to get so bad that companies began hanging signs which read "No soliciting" or "Please do not bother our agents." Or "We have our own in-house closing company." And yet, I knew there was a monsoon of business behind these signs... if I could just get past them.

Frustrated, and thinking I had tried everything, I suddenly had a thought. While I knew that it was tough for me to get in to see potential clients, it was really easy for them to come see me, if only they had a good reason. That was the easy part. Now I just had to come up with that reason.

In truth, I didn't come up with the reason. It actually ended up appearing on its own. A local paper got wind of my book *Getting Loaded* and did a story on me. A small paper indeed, but nonetheless, I hit the front page of the business section.

Shortly after this front page debut, I popped into a real estate office and an agent actually said to me, "Hey, I read about you in the paper. I didn't know you were an author."

"You're an author?" Said another agent trying to send a fax.

"Yes I am," I said to the two agents who hardly gave me the time of day a couple of weeks ago.

As we began talking I noticed the familiar "No Soliciting" sign in the window. But this time I wasn't soliciting. *They* were asking me questions about publishing. *They* wanted me around.

"Ya know," said one agent, "I've been working on this book for a few years now, I just never knew how to sell it. How did you do it?"

"I'm happy to send you the query letter I sent to get a literary agent," I said. I quickly followed with, "Can I have one of your cards?"

The business card I had been chasing for weeks effortlessly landed in my hands.

"That would be great," said the agent. "And I know you've been in here dropping off brochures about your closing company. I'll take a look at that. I got a deal that's happening in your neck of the woods and I'll try to send it your way."

Often times when we try to network, we feel we need to approach it head on. We want to sell a real estate service to a real estate agent, so we walk straight into the real estate office and ask for the order. This is all well and good, but *everyone* who has a real estate service to sell is using the same approach.

I learned from my stint at this company that not only do I need to be the person who people want to come to, but that people may come to me because of a reason I had never thought of, and for a reason that has nothing to do with what I am actually selling.

When I was banging on doors asking for real estate business, I wasn't new and interesting. I wasn't anyone these real estate agents wanted to meet because, frankly, I was just like everyone else. But as an author, I was new and different.

Networking is like trying to get thru a locked door. Sure you can keep trying to kick the door in, but it's easier if the person on the other side unlocks it. You just need to give them the reason. So, if you're trying to connect with someone on a certain level, maybe a good idea would be to switch levels. For instance, if you're trying to sell your financial advising services, maybe the way to get that new client is to start talking about sports. Or mention you're a wine expert. Or a semi-professional tennis player. The whole trick to guerrilla networking is to find the *easiest connection point, even if its not the ideal connection point at the moment.*

Just focus on connecting at the easiest level — at a level where they want to meet you — and then build from there. And how do you know what the easiest level is? Just ask them. And listen! If you're selling used cars but they're talking about their daughter in the Girl Scouts, you might want to stop trying to connect on the subject of used cars... and start connecting by talking about the Girl Scouts.

AUTHOR BIOGRAPHY: Peter G. Bielagus is one of the few licensed financial advisors in the country who specializes exclusively on Young America. Peter gives over 60 talks each year to students and young professionals showing them how to jumpstart their financial lives. In addition to speaking *to* Young America, Peter also speaks *about* Young America. He shows parents, corporations and educators how to get young people excited about money management. He is the author of *Getting Loaded: Make A Million, While You're Still Young Enough To Enjoy It*, published internationally by Penguin Putnam/NAL. He also wrote *The Freeway Guide to Personal Finance*, an 80-minute audio CD distributed by freewayguides.com. Peter also created *The Complete Financial Life Kit for Young America*, the only financial course that focuses exclusively on the challenges of Young America. Peter is a frequent guest on TV and radio shows nationwide and he has been featured in several of the nation's premier publications such as *The Wall Street Journal*, *The Miami Herald* and *USA Today*.

Young America's Financial Coach

170 South River Rd

Bedford, NH 03110

(603) 606-5685

(603) 673-0080 fax

www.peterbspeaks.com

www.financiallifekit.com

peter@peterbspeaks.com

MONROE MANN:

...or, how I convinced all of these wonderful people to contribute to this book

Jay Levinson — I (Monroe) wrote a book, sent Jay a copy, and followed up (four years later — bad Monroe!) via email before deploying to Iraq. **He wanted to meet me because** I'm a good writer, a guerrilla marketer, and was deploying to Iraq in service to my country. **I wanted to meet him because** he is the god of marketing.

Ned Vizzini — I was playing guitar and singing in the subways of New York City and one night, as I was counting the money I made that night, I saw a business card. It was Ned's, from the newspaper, *NY Press*. I emailed him, and he replied, "Oh, I'm a music reviewer for the paper. If I left my card with you, it's because I liked what I heard you playing." Soon, we both found out we were published authors, and he actually ended up playing bass in my band *Running for Famous* for a while. **He wanted to meet me because** he liked my music. **I wanted to meet him because** he could potentially bring publicity to my band and musical endeavors.

Andrew Young — I deployed to Iraq with Andrew. He was my superior officer on our team: I was the second in command of a four-man team whose mission was to train and advise the fourth Iraqi Army on matters of intelligence and military policing. **He wanted to meet me because** I was an intelligence officer assigned to the same 14-man MITT team (Military Transition Team). **I wanted to meet him** for the same reasons. Military brothers stick together.

Carol Blaha — I met Carol through Jay, Mitch Meyerson, & Al Lautenslager — all of the Guerrilla Marketing Coaching certification program. Carol is a fellow Guerrilla Marketing coach. **She wanted to meet me because** I offered her an opportunity to get word out about her services through a contribution to this book. **I wanted to meet her because** her story would provide a unique perspective to readers.

Arthur Brown — He read my book, *The Theatrical Juggernaut*, years ago, then took my class, and then became a client of mine. I like him so much that I asked him to be a part of this book. **He wanted to meet me because** he felt I could help him with his acting career, and because he too was a published author. **I wanted to meet him because** he was funny, charming, and I felt he has what it takes to 'make it'.

James Dillehay — I met James through Jay, Mitch, & Al. James is a fellow Guerrilla Marketing coach and like me, is contributing to the book, *Guerrilla Marketing on the Front Lines*. **He wanted to meet me because** I offered him an opportunity to get word out about his new book through a contribution to this book. **I wanted to meet him because** his story would provide a unique perspective to readers.

Barry Morgenstein — I met Barry because he took some head-shots for me last year. **He wanted to meet me because** I was a potential client, a combat veteran, and because I had a large network of actors, artists, athletes, and celebrities to whom I could potentially introduce him. **I wanted to meet him because** I like the work he had done for others, and needed some new headshots.

Kathy Hagenbuch — I met Kathy through Jay, Mitch, & Al. Kathy too is a fellow Guerrilla Marketing coach. **She wanted to meet me because** I offered her an opportunity to get word out about her services through a contribution to this book. **I wanted to meet her because** her story would provide a unique perspective to readers.

Debbie Bordelon — She found an ad that I had taken out for myself in *Premiere Magazine* — something I had done in hopes of keeping my fanbase alive while deployed to Iraq. She emailed me, became a fan, and that's all she wrote. **She wanted to meet me because** she was impressed with all I had done, for both myself, and our country. **I wanted to meet her because** anyone who was such an amazing fan just *had* to be cool — heck, she even sent me care packages while I was in Iraq. Thanks Debbie!

Graham Guerra — I became a certified Guerrilla Marketing coach, and in so doing, was invited to contribute to the new book, *Guerrilla Marketing on the Front Lines.* One of my fellow contributors said she knew some people in the film business and the arts who I might want to connect with. Her name was Mary Scarborough, and one of her sons was Graham Guerra. She gave me his number and prepped the battlefield with a referral, and when I called, he was already expecting my call. We became friends, and I asked him to be a part of the book. **He wanted to meet me because** Mary referred me, and because I was affiliated with Jay Levinson. **I wanted to meet him because** he was a cool guy, very approachable, and quite unpretentious given his stature in the art world. He also knows Keith Ferrazzi, haha (but I found that out later.)

Ashley Ann Serafin — I met Ashley through one of my free business seminars. She became a client, then later read my book. **She wanted to meet me because** she figured I could help her with her career. **I wanted to meet her because** she had a glow about her, has an uncanny resemblance to Drew Barrymore, and has great ambition, just like me.

Knox Vanderpool — I met Knox at the 2006 pro-wakeboarding tour stop in Acworth, GA in May of that year. I was down there location scouting, and meeting the various players in the wakeboarding industry in preparation for shooting my upcoming film, *In the Wake.* I saw Knox's 'booth' set up on the beach, immediately fell in love with the SAYiWON'T concept, bought a t-shirt, and kept in touch. **He wanted to meet me because** I was the producer of what is soon to be the world's first wakeboarding feature film, and his clothing line could get great publicity by being associated with it. **I wanted to meet him because** the mastermind behind such a novel, invigorating, and inspirational concept *had* to be worth meeting.

Paul Rieckhoff — I went to Officer Candidate School with him at Empire State Military Academy/Regional Training Institute at Camp Smith, NY. Just as he was returning from Iraq, I was shipping out. We've obviously kept in touch. **He wanted to meet me because** we had the shared experience of that grueling ordeal known as Officer Candidate School. **I wanted to meet him** for the same reasons. Military brothers stick together.

Bones Rodriguez — He read my book, liked what I had to say, and we've since been friends. **He wanted to meet me because** I was a mover and shaker, like him, in show business, and because I too felt the need to help others become more successful. **I wanted to meet him** for the very same reasons.

Dennis Hurley — He read my book, *The Theatrical Juggernaut*, became a client of Unstoppable Artists, and soon a friend. **He wanted to meet me because** he knew about the crazy publicity stunts and marketing miracles I have helped other clients with. **I wanted to meet him because** I see myself when I look at the things he is doing, and how he does them.

Phil Malandrino — I met Phil during auditions for my film *Origami Deathmatch*. At first, there was no part for him, but I liked him so much, I quickly wrote a part for him, and soon,

I also made him my second assistant director. Now, we are collaborating on a number of film projects. **He wanted to meet me because** he felt that I was a young version of himself, and because he had always wanted to get involved in show business; he felt that I was going somewhere in the business, and wanted to be associated with me. **I wanted to meet him because** he has a work ethic as strong as mine, was the first person on set and the last person to leave set (with me), and because I felt he would be a huge asset to all of my future film productions.

Douglas C. Williams — I met Doug through my class. After taking my class, he went on a publicity, marketing, and advertising rampage... and one I am quite proud of. **He wanted to meet me because** I offered a fresh perspective on what it takes to make it in show business, the arts, and publishing. **I wanted to meet him because** I thought it was cool that he was a former minor league baseball player, and that he was taking that drive and putting it towards success in the arts.

Roberta Muse — I met Bobbie at Fryeburg Academy... as her French student in the mid nineties. **She wanted to meet me because** I was one of her 'star' French students who went on to become reasonably fluent in the language, who still speaks it today, and who loves her for introducing me to the language. **I wanted to meet her because** she was my first true fan outside of my family, because she supported me as an actor when everyone else didn't, and because she was one of the few 'friends' who took the time to write to me during basic training with the US Army (one of the most diffi-cult challenges of my life.)

Kip Gienau — I met Kip through Jay Levinson, Mitch Meyerson, and Al Lautenslager. Kip is a fellow Guerrilla Marketing coach. **He wanted to meet me because** we share a simi-lar love of networking, and because his ad agency is not too far from where I live. **I wanted to meet him because** he has a very prestigious advertising agency, and I was looking for someone to help out with some television ads I had been developing.

Marcia Harp — She saw an ad for my company in Michael Levine's LBN e-lert, checked out my website, liked what she saw, and called me. She soon became a client. And for you sports fans out there, her nephew is the head coach for the Miami Dolphins. Coolio, eh? **She wanted to meet me because** — in her words — "I just knew when I read that ad that you were someone I was destined to work with. I could tell that you were different from everyone else, and from every other coach out there." **I wanted to meet her because** anyone who says that — sincerely — makes me smile, and because her great big heart came shooting out from the telephone when I spoke with her.

Scott duPont — He had read my book, *The Theatrical Juggernaut*, and when I was down in Florida doing some loca-tion scouting for my wakeboarding film, he invited me to a big to-do with local actors, filmmakers, and producers, where I finally met him in person. He asked me to stand up, and he gave me a very warm introduction to over 100 attendees... who then wanted to meet me. **Scott himself wanted to meet me because** he feels my book should be required reading for every actor and artist in the world who wants to get ahead. **I wanted to meet him because** he had a number of successful films under his belt, and because he was the president of the Florida Motion Picture and Television Association.

Kolie Krutcher — He came to a free business seminar I was teaching, subsequently became a client, and then read my book. **He wanted to meet me because** he correctly assumed I could get his writing, showbusiness, and speaking career up and running quickly. **I wanted to meet him because** I could tell that he was going to become one of my star clients.

Ed Smith — He found me in RTIR, the Radio Television Interview Report, where I had advertised. He asked me to be a guest on his television show, and we have since become friends. I called him up and asked him to contribute. **He wanted to meet me because** I seemed like a great guest for his show. **I wanted to meet him because** I wanted to be on his show.

Scott Norman — He read my book, *The Theatrical Juggernaut*, then became a client when he moved to New York City. I asked him to contribute to this book. **He wanted to meet me because** he knew I was going places and wanted to learn from me. **I wanted to meet him because** I knew he was going places and wanted to help him.

Peter Bielagus — I attended a college booking convention where public speakers go to get booked on the college circuit. Peter was one of the speakers, as was I, and we ended up speaking to one another on the last day of the event. We've since kept in touch. **He wanted to meet me because** I was a fellow speaker, and also because of my connections and experience in Hollywood (he has a finance-based television show in the works.) **I wanted to meet him because** he was my age, really cool, and made his entire living by speaking at colleges: I figured I could learn something from him.

AUTHOR BIOGRAPHY: Monroe Mann is the founder of Unstoppable Artists in Manhattan, a combat veteran of Operation Iraqi Freedom, the lead singer of the seven-piece ROMP band *Running for Famous*, the author of a number of books, and the co-star, screenwriter, and producer of a bunch of films including *Origami Deathmatch*, *Hollywood Combat*, and *In the Wake*. His contact information can be found at the beginning of this book.

PART 4

Creating Your Own Guerrilla Networking Strategy... in 10 Easy Steps

INTRODUCTION:
Creating Your Own Guerrilla Networking Strategy... in 10 Easy Steps

Okay, now that you fully understand what guerrilla networking is, it's time for the fun part: putting together your *own* guerrilla networking strategy.

While it's true that some people stumble onto a guerrilla networking strategy by accident, if you truly want to put the odds in your favor, you should consider a planned and well-thought-out guerrilla networking strategy just as important as a planned guerrilla *marketing* strategy.

To be sure, the concept of guerrilla networking is simple: just become the type of person other people want to meet. The crux of this task is in the *how*. And that's exactly what this part of the book is about: helping you to assemble a strategy that outlines precisely and methodically how *you* are going to become the type of person others want to meet. Is your strategy going to be simple to grasp? Yes. Is it going to be easy to execute? Nope. Guerrilla networking is not a 'quick fix'; it is a long-term strategy that you need to embrace fully or don't even bother wasting the time.

It's only going to take you 20 minutes to put your initial guerrilla networking strategy down on paper, ready to put into action. The big question, though, is: *will* you put it into action?

If you say, "Yes!" — Let's get started.

THE STRATEGY —
Step by Step

1 **STEP ONE:** Create a list on a piece of paper of all of the people who *you* would like to meet, work with, work for, or become friends with. To begin, just start with five or 10 people, so that you learn the process.

EXAMPLE:

Bill Gates

Keanu Reeves

Avril Lavigne

Hilary Duff

Tony Hawk

Jack Nicholson

2 **STEP TWO:** Take each of these names and put one each at the top of a piece of blank paper. In other words, if you wrote down five names, you'll need five pieces of paper, each with a name at the top of it.

EXAMPLE:

Bill Gates	Keanu Reeves	Avril Lavigne

Hilary Duff	Tony Hawk	Jack Nicholson

3 **STEP THREE**: This is the 'why' phase of the guerrilla networking process. *Why* would this person want to meet you? What type of person do you need to become for this person to consider you worthy of his time? What qualities might this person find attractive.

There are really only two ways for you to entice others into wanting to meet you: the first is to *fill in the gaps* (i.e. determine what that person wants but lacks) and the second is to realize that *like attracts like* (i.e. determine all the positive characteristics of the person you want to meet, and then emulate them).

So, underneath each name, make two columns:

On the LEFT column (the 'what I can do to entice him to meet me/fill in the gaps' column), list as many different reasons why this person might like to meet you, or the type of person he might like to meet, i.e. for Jack Nicholson, you might list: Win an Oscar; Write a screenplay; Write him a letter; Invest money in one of his films; Become his friend; etc. You might also list particular people, for example: Someone who likes horse racing; Stephen Spielberg; a successful movie director; a screenwriter with a role written just for him; a beautiful and young 20-something woman; or someone who has $20 million to invest in his new film.

On the RIGHT column (the 'what type of person would this person want to meet/like attracts like' column), make a comprehensive list all of the characteristics, accomplishments, and interests of/about this person that you find most attractive. Some of the items on your list might read: Successful; Accomplished; Rebel; Millionaire; Dangerous; Wild Charming Smile; Personable; etc.

EXAMPLE:

Jack Nicholson — WHY WOULD THIS

What Can I Do To Entice Him To Meet Me?
FILL IN THE GAPS

-Win an Oscar

-Write a screenplay

-Write him a letter

-Invest money in one of his films

-Become or introduce him to someone who likes horse racing

-Become friends with Stephen Spielberg

-Become or introduce him to a big movie director

-Become or introduce him to a screenwriter with a role written just for him

-Introduce him to a beautiful and young twenty-something woman

-Become or introduce him to someone who wants to invest $20 million in his next film

ERSON WANT TO MEET ME?

What Type Of Person Would This Person Want to Meet?
LIKE ATTRACTS LIKE

Someone who (like him):

-Is successful

-Is accomplished

-Is a rebel

-Is a millionaire

-Is dangerous

-Has a wild charming smile

-Is personable

-Takes on strange film roles

-Likes boats

4 **STEP FOUR:** This is the 'how' phase of guerrilla networking planning. For every 'why' response (i.e. every single phrase written underneath someone's name that explains WHY this person would want to meet you), write that 'why' by itself at the top of another fresh piece of paper. For instance, in step three, our first 'why' turned out to be 'Win an Oscar'. So, put 'Win an Oscar' on the top of a new piece of paper, and then ask yourself, 'How?' Ask yourself, "Okay, winning an Oscar is one of my guerrilla networking goals because others will then want to meet me. So then, *how* am I actually going to win that Oscar?" Taking another example, this time from the right column, the first entry was, 'Successful'. So ask yourself, "Okay, becoming more successful is one of my guerrilla networking goals because then others will want to meet me. So then, how am I actually going to become more successful?"

EXAMPLE:

> Win An Oscar —
> HOW AM I GOING TO DO IT?
>
> –
> –
> –
> –
> –

```
┌─────────────────────────────────────────────┐
│     Become Successful —                       │
│   HOW AM I GOING TO DO IT?                    │
├─────────────────────────────────────────────┤
│  –                                            │
│                                               │
│  –                                            │
│                                               │
│  –                                            │
│                                               │
│  –                                            │
│                                               │
│  –                                            │
│                                               │
└─────────────────────────────────────────────┘
```

STEP FIVE: Now, as you ask yourself the 'how' questions, start writing down whatever answers come to mind. If we still are using 'winning an Oscar' as an example, a possible initial list could read: get cast in an Oscar-caliber role; write an Oscar-caliber screenplay; produce an Oscar-caliber film; write an Oscar-caliber soundtrack; and the list goes on. If the 'why' were 'Write him a letter', then our hows might read: find his address; figure out what to write him; contact his agents and managers; find out something personal about him that might entice him to write me back. Since one of the 'why' responses was 'Successful', the list of hows for that item might read: make more money; become published; get a writeup in a newspaper; take more risks; develop more friendships with people who are more successful than I am; etc.

EXAMPLE:

> ## Win An Oscar —
> ## HOW AM I GOING TO DO IT?
>
> -get cast in an Oscar-caliber role
>
> -write an Oscar-caliber screenplay
>
> -produce an Oscar-caliber film
>
> *...and keep adding to this list*

> ## Write Him a Letter —
> ## HOW AM I GOING TO DO IT?
>
> -find his address
>
> -figure out what to write him
>
> -contact his agents and managers
>
> *...and keep adding to this list*

STEP SIX: Continue to break down each 'how' even more. The idea is to break down each of the hows into small and manageable tasks — absurdly small — for otherwise, you won't do find the time to do them. For instance, the 'how' of getting cast in an Oscar-caliber role is still pretty lofty and way too 'big' to tackle. So, break it down even more: get affiliated with a prestigious acting program; become friends with the top five feature film casting directors in Hollywood; become represented by one of the top six talent agencies in Hollywood; get cast in a film from an up-and-coming Oscar-caliber director, screenwriter, or producer. And then, break each one of those tasks down even more.

EXAMPLE *(using two of the 'how's I came up with earlier)*:

Win An Oscar — HOW AM I GOING TO DO IT?

-Get cast in an Oscar-caliber role
 	
• Get affiliated with the most prestigious acting program in the world
 	
   * Buy Backstage
 	
   * Do Research Online
 	
• Become friends with the top five casting directors in Hollywood

* Buy Ross Reports to Find Out Who They Are

* Decide What Types of Flowers To Send

- Get cast in a film from an up-and-coming Oscar-caliber director, screenwriter, or producer

  * Get An Agent To Submit Me For Big Roles

  * Produce My Own Film That Shows My Talent

-Write an Oscar-caliber screenplay

- Learn how to write a screenplay

  * Take a screenwriting class

  * Buy screenwriting books

- Come up with the idea

  * Make a list of 20 ideas for screenplays

  * Read magazines to get ideas

- Get the screenplay in front of him

  * Find out his favorite restaurant

  * Call his manager and make a pitch

Write Him a Letter —
HOW AM I GOING TO DO IT?

-Find his address

- Go to IMDBPro.com

  * Get a subscription

  * Write his representation's address down

- Go to ContactAnyCelebrity.com

  * Get Subscription

  * Write his address down

- Go to WhoRepresents.com

  * Get a subscription

  * Write his representation's address down

-Figure out what to write him

- Determine some personal things about him

  * Do a Google search for his name

  * Go watch all of his movies

- Find someone who has worked with him

  * Ask any of your acting friends

* If you don't have acting friends, make some!
• Determine what you want from him
  * Make a list of all of your current projects
  * Figure out what you can give him in return for his help

7 **STEP SEVEN:** Repeat steps four, five, and six until each how is 'immediately doable'. By immediately doable, all we mean is that you can do each task in five minutes or less. If it takes you longer than five minutes to do something on your list, then that task is too big. Keep breaking each how down until you have created a monster-size task list of **simple things that are** *immediately doable* for every person on your list.

8 **STEP EIGHT:** *DO THEM! DO THEM! LOOK AT YOUR LIST AND START DOING THOSE THINGS THAT ARE GOING TO TURN YOU INTO THE TYPE OF PERSON THOSE VERY PEOPLE YOU LISTED IN STEP ONE ARE GOING TO WANT TO MEET!* (In case you didn't realize, this step is absolutely the most important step of all.)

9 STEP NINE: Go back to Step One, adding more people to your original list, and work through each of the steps once again. While working step-by-step through your new list, always refine each step for previous guerrilla networking 'targets' along the way. Note: Your 'guerrilla networking Targets' are those people who you are targeting to meet — but not by actually trying to meet them, but rather, by becoming the person *they* want to meet.

10 STEP 10: Repeat all of these steps constantly, every day, without fail. Realize that even if you don't end up accomplishing the ultimate objective you set out to achieve, by approaching your life in this manner, you are inevitably going to become a more interesting, diverse, and accomplished individual... and that is worth any effort. Just making the effort may be enough to entice the people you want to meet to give you a call.

Oh, and by the way: while you're busy implementing these steps, why don't you take a moment to show someone else how to create their own guerrilla networking strategy, now that you know how to do it. By helping others become more successful, you are — once again — becoming the type of person other people want to meet.

BONUS EXERCISE ONE: Think of five things that are special about you RIGHT NOW that might entice someone into wanting to meet you TOMORROW. Think of five MORE things. Continue adding to this list daily. Always remember that it doesn't matter if *you* think some quality about you is cool; all that matters is that someone *else* might think it's cool. For example, you may have grown up in Maine your whole life and never left the state, or even the country. You might think your life is pretty boring, but to someone who has been jetsetting around the world his whole life... your life might actually be pretty intriguing. As another example, you might be a member of a family of lawyers and be really bored mentioning it to people, but to someone who is looking for a lawyer, your family could be the answer to her prayers. Make sense? If you get stuck, *ask other people the same question.*

BONUS EXERCISE TWO: Take inventory of your own life, and ask yourself how desirable you currently are, how desirable you want to be, and most importantly, how you are going to bridge that gap. Then do it.

BONUS EXERCISE THREE: Do something cool, *right now*. Then, get really crazy... and tell everyone you meet — even perfect strangers — what you just did.

BONUS EXERCISE FOUR: Never rest on your laurels. Always be thinking. Evolving. Developing. Different. *Always* be different. VERY different. In a good way.

BONUS EXERCISE FIVE: Write your book already! It should have been published yesterday! And if you're already published, what are you waiting for? Write and publish a *new* book!

CONCLUSION

Guerrilla networking is a simple concept to understand. But its simplicity is also its curse. Because people 'get' the concept so quickly, many people incorrectly believe that it's not necessary to work at it, or feel that it's far too 'simple' to warrant any effort expended to put it into practice.

So, while the concept may be easy to 'get', you absolutely must understand that it is something that can take many months for you to really grasp, many years before you truly start to see its magnificent results, and perhaps a lifetime to master.

That established, if it takes so long to really start to see the results, why do it then? Here's a quick story to answer that question, and you may have heard it before: An old man is browsing at a bookstore, and passes by the music section. While passing by, he notices a 'Teach Yourself Piano' book, and suddenly sees another man browsing through a more advanced book on music theory. The old man sighs, "Oh, how I wish I could play piano. But can you imagine how old I'd be by the time I learned?" The man — who turned out to be a piano teacher — replied, "Yes, I do know how old you will be by the time you learn how to play piano — the same age you'll be if you don't."

In other words, commit *today* to becoming a guerrilla networker — to becoming the type of person other people want to meet.

The key is to constantly ask yourself on a daily basis: what more can I be doing — or be doing differently — to entice other people (the very people I want to meet) to want to meet me?

But answering that question is only half the battle. You can't just answer the question, and then ignore the answer's advice; that will doom you to struggle. Avoid that! You must act on the answers! If you do, the world will be your oyster.

For example, if after you ask the above question, you determine that you need to run for office — *do that!* If you determine you need to go back to school and get more education — *do that!* If you determine that you need to join the military, write a book, start a band, launch a company, gain publicity, or even walk on the moon — *do that!* Make the commitment to start the transformation TODAY. Every day, take another step towards becoming that very person of value and accomplishment you know other people would want to meet. Become a true guerrilla networker.

No, it's not rocket science, but truth be told, becoming a rocket scientist would *definitely* entice others to want to meet you. That's guerrilla networking — because it makes others want to meet you. Doing great things for your fellow man would also entice others to want to meet you. Helping the underdog would have the same result. So would inventing something amazing. So would writing a blockbuster Hollywood screenplay. Heck, so would the simple act of saying, "Thank you," to someone — which you probably don't say often enough.

Bottom line: how well guerrilla networking works for you is directly related to how much effort you are willing to exert to *become* that type of person other people want to meet. It ain't easy folks. And yes, it could very well take years — as it has for me, Monroe. So be it. As the old man above learned, you're going to get older anyway, so why not develop yourself as much as you can along the way?

Jay & I truly do look forward to meeting you. Why is that? Precisely because by reading this book, you have taken the first steps towards becoming the type of person that we wish to meet.

~Monroe Mann & Jay Conrad Levinson

For more info about guerrilla networking, check out:
www.StopMeetingPeople.com

APPENDIX 1:
Recommended Reading List

BOOKS ON NETWORKING

Never Eat Alone by Keith Ferrazzi

Dig Your Well Before Your Thirsty by Harvey Mackay

Power Schmoozing by Terri Mandell

Power Networking by Donna Fisher & Sandy Vilas

Networking Smart by Wayne E. Baker

Working the Room by Nick Morgan

Opening Closed Doors — Keys to Reaching Hard-to-Reach People by C. Richard Weylman

BOOKS BY JAY LEVINSON

Guerrilla Marketing, 4th Edition

Mastering Guerrilla Marketing

Guerrilla Marketing for Free

Guerilla Marketing Attack

Guerrilla Advertising

& over 30 more!

BOOKS BY MONROE MANN

The Theatrical Juggernaut

Battle Cries for the Underdog

To Benning & Back

The Artist's MBA (**Coming Soon**)

Operation: STARDOM! (**Coming Soon**)

Learning How to Juggle — Time Management Skills of the Stars (**Coming Soon**)

APPENDIX 2:
Networking Resources

a. Jay Levinson's Guerrilla Marketing Association

GET YOUR FREE GIFT!

Until now, no marketing association in existence could make a business bulletproof. But once again, Jay Conrad Levinson, the most respected marketer in the world, has broken new ground. The Guerrilla Marketing Association is quite literally a blueprint for business immortality.

Receive a two-month **FREE** trial membership in the Guerrilla Marketing Association where Guerrilla Marketing coaches and leading business experts answer your business questions online and during exclusive weekly telephone chats. **This $99 value is your gift** for investing in *Guerrilla Networking*.

Join right now before your competition does at:
www.Morgan-James.com/gma

To purchase additional Guerrilla Marketing products by Jay Conrad Levinson, visit the Morgan James Publishing Bookstore at www.MorganJamesPublishing.com.

b. Monroe Mann's Juggernaut Club

FREE TRIAL MEMBERSHIP!

In case you don't know what a juggernaut is: it's an absolutely unstoppable force.

The Juggernaut Club is a networking success group, partly based online (through a highly interactive online environment), and partly operated via phone (every month, we have an inspiring group teleconference with members from around the world.)

The point of the group? We help each other become more successful through shared motivation, inspiration, business tips, contacts, and collaboration.

If you are interested in becoming involved with this burgeoning network of winners from around the world and from all walks of life, simply contact Monroe Mann, and he'd be pleased to discuss with you further.

For more information about membership in this elite group, please visit:

www.UnstoppableArtists.com or
www.TheJClub.net

c. Monroe Mann's American Break Diving Association

Break Diving® is the lost art of finding and creating opportunity.
Break diving leaves nothing to chance.
Luck? There's no such thing.
I am a break diver... and I will find a way.

Instead of waiting for opportunities to float to the surface, break divers plunge right into the cold and icy waters of resistance and find those breaks & opportunities themselves.

The American Break Diving Association is a collective group of winners who live by the Break Diver's Creed — *No Rules, No Excuses, No Regrets®*. We draw our membership from every corner of the world, and would love to have you join our ranks.

The breaks are there for the diving... So go get 'em!

For more information about membership in this elite group, please visit:
www.UnstoppableArtists.com or
www.BreakDiving.com

d. Guerrilla Networking Central

For more information about the philosophy of guerrilla networking, check out the official site at:

www.StopMeetingPeople.com